Winegums from The Telegram

A regular online essayist for five years, Johnny Monroe in his alter-ego guise of 'Petunia Winegum' has managed to provoke thought, debate and discussion by documenting events of the day with a satirical, critical eye and the odd side-splitting turn-of-phrase. His good fortune is to be writing in an era stripped of certainties, a turbulent, Stygian interregnum in which no waspish wordsmith worth his salt can bemoan the absence of inspiration or dearth of source material.

From the combative cockpit of cyberspace to the printed page at last, here is the first volume of Johnny Monroe's collected essays from the 'Winegum Telegram' blog – covering everything from the political to the pop cultural whilst refusing to recognise either side of the divide as exclusive copyright-holders of the moral high-ground. Outside the tent pissing-in, Monroe's detached perspective allows for a clearer picture of the most unpredictable (and occasionally mind-boggling) period in living memory than can be found on Fleet Street, especially when it comes to *the* contentious British issue of the age – Brexit.

Divided into three distinctive chapters, this inaugural volume of what could well become a wider series highlights the advantages of the author having the freedom to set his own remit. A cast of characters may include the anticipated – Boris Johnson, Jeremy Corbyn, Nigel Farage *et al;* but there are also appearances from the likes of Scott Walker, Albert Finney and Kurt Cobain. All of human life is here – well, a fair slice of it; and along with a sardonic look at the public figures whose presence on the front pages of everyone's lives makes them unavoidable targets for scrutiny, there are just as many poignant studies of a uniquely personal nature that nonetheless touch a universal nerve.

Drawing in the main from Monroe's 2018/19 articles, 'Winegums from The Telegram' selects primarily British obsessions, so those in search of stinging portraits of Putin and Trump or topics of a more global nature would be better off waiting for volume two, if and when it appears. In the meantime, sample a subjective, contemporary time capsule as England swings to the beat of an exceedingly divisive drum...

Winegums from The Telegram

Essays and stuff by
Johnny Monroe

1
Village Idiots

Westminster, Brexit and beyond the bubble

DIVIDE AND MISRULE
30 January 2019

One of the many reasons why I have drifted away from the daily missives some of you used to look forward to is that I don't talk politics with anyone anymore. Conversations that spawned and informed many a past post on here no longer take place due to unforeseen circumstances that have led to a loss of appetite for many things, never mind talking politics. Nobody I now know is as clued-up as some I used to know, so I tend to get asked questions about what's going on as though I'm some expert oracle of the kind Michael Gove would no doubt despise; that in itself would be a good enough reason to be one, but I'm not, alas. At the same time, I've broken my blog silence without any advance planning simply because my sedated, slumbering inner blogger has been stirred back into action through sheer exasperation.

I guess I don't have to elaborate on what motivated this unscheduled return to the frontline. Yes, I've followed events like the rest of you of late – the BBC News Channel, 'Peston', 'This Week', the programme formerly known as 'The Daily Politics', and that bastion of outrageous institutionalised bigotry that won't even allow MPs fond of playing the race card when their myriad shortcomings are exposed to drone on forever, 'Question Time'. So hapless have I become in trying to locate any light at the end of the Brexit tunnel that all I could conclude from a recent 'Newsnight' debate on the subject was the undeniable fact that 65 year-old Baroness Meyer has a great pair of legs. Yes, I'm that f****d. But angry as well. I know I'm not alone there; perhaps this country's defining characteristic at the moment is anger, though it's no real wonder when our elected representatives make one yearn for the intervention of Guy Fawkes and his pals.

OK, let's start at the top. Theresa May is perhaps the most nihilistically intransigent Prime Minister since Ted Heath, yet like the equally toe-curling portrayal of a certain Time Lord by Jodie Whittaker, our Glorious Leader tries to draw on her predecessors to create her own interpretation of a part she lacks the talent to make her own. She combines the blinkered, deluded cluelessness of Cameron with the bloody-minded tunnel vision of Thatcher in her Poll Tax death-throes, and blends the excruciatingly uncomfortable, awkward-on-camera bumbling of Gordon Brown with the God-bothering righteousness of Blair at his most sanctimoniously evangelical. She seems to have the knack of taking on the worst characteristics of past PMs, and as a result she's even got people feeling sorry for her, just like they feel sorry for every tone-deaf wannabe being ripped to shreds by the judges on TV talent shows. What an achievement that is, to win the favour of the electorate by courting their pity.

Never mind – Mrs May and her unruly Cabinet of careerists, crawlers and backstabbers will soon be overthrown by the Great Socialist Revolution of the Messiah, an event which has had more postponements than HS2. Oh, God. What a choice we face – dumb or dumber. Yet there's always the prospect of a Third Party, of course, an SDP for the twenty-first century composed of all those Honourable Members who are largely responsible for the mess we're in. Yes, those (© John Major) 'bastards' who have made it their daily duty to thwart the outcome of a democratic vote they didn't want and didn't expect. Whether it's Chuka Remoaner and the rest of the Miliband deadwood or the likes of Anna 'Nazi' Soubry, the two and-a-half years since the *actual* People's Vote have been defined in Parliament by this contemptible coterie of detached demagogues deliberately throwing down obstacle after obstacle in order to prevent the enacting of something a majority of the electorate voted for. To put it plainly, they are despicable.

I admit I voted Remain in 2016, motivated by a 'better the devil you know' approach rather than any particular affection for an organisation I honestly hadn't really given much thought to. Since then, however, my perspective has undergone a radical transformation entirely due to those who voted the same way as me. I have been appalled by the attitude and behaviour of some of those who advocated Remain and their foot-stamping refusal to accept a result that told them what they didn't want to hear. Their superior arrogance has only been matched by the superior arrogance of the EU itself. No wonder they're such kindred spirits.

To me, it now seems the reasons behind the result of the EU Referendum of 2016 have distinct parallels with the circumstances that put Donald Trump in the White House. The outcome was the consequence of so many people feeling so powerless after being ignored and dismissed for decades, whether by the scythe Thatcher took to communities dependent on heavy industry or the Coalition's ruthless austerity policies. Suddenly, the powerless were presented with a platform to give the powers-that-be that had trampled them underfoot for generations a legally sanctioned bloody nose. MSM talking heads can waffle on about immigration or every other explanation given for the result, but in the end, Brexit was the most gloriously defiant 'fuck you' aimed at the political class in post-war British history. That's the way it seems to me now, anyway. And the subsequent response of the political class and their media sponsors has only strengthened this opinion.

Just a couple of weeks ago, that nasty old guillotine-knitter Polly Toynbee reiterated the jaw-dropping narrative of

Remoaners at their most vile by openly wishing death upon anyone over 50 who voted Leave in order that Youth would inherit the vote. This narrative of course assumes anyone who wasn't eligible to vote in 2016 would naturally vote Remain in the event of a second Referendum. Yes, I've no doubt all the 'young people' Polly Toynbee and her fellow Grauniad scribes probably come into contact with – at a guess, the student offspring of their affluent acquaintances – probably *would* vote Remain; but what of the products of *under-privilege* in every grotty corner of the country who are tumbling out of an educational bubble trashed by useless Blairite rhetoric and straight into zero-hours uncertainty or the Circumlocution Office maze of Universal Credit? Why should they automatically give the thumbs-up to the system that exists to make their lives a misery? The great divide in Great Britain is the same today as it has always been – not gender, not colour, not creed, but class.

Yes, I know I'm guilty of generalising here. If Leave was an entirely working-class upsurge, how does that explain Jacob Rees-Mogg? Maybe he gets so much air-time because he helps reinforce the MSM view that Leave voters are all either eccentric, vaguely unhinged toffs like the Honourable Member for North East Somerset and Boris, or red-faced gammon men in yellow vests to whom Tommy Robinson is Che Guevara. Dehumanising your enemy is the first rule in the book of warfare, and the populace has been battered by a sustained campaign of dehumanisation by the powerful Remoaner mafia since June 2016, something that continues to this very day with the Project Fear prediction of martial law, absent medicines, empty supermarket shelves and a future Britain resembling that of the BBC's mid-70s Dystopian drama, 'Survivors'.

In many respects I wish the Referendum had never happened. I think it has been disastrous for the country's (admittedly shaky) concept of unity, but at the same time has served to highlight divisions that have been in place for far longer than most were prepared to admit. There is no easy answer and there is no easy outcome, but if the will of the majority is denied, the contract between electorate and elected will be broken forever. And God knows what happens then. Be careful out there...

THE SHITEHOUSE DECLARATION
18 February 2019

As tribute acts go, I've probably seen worse, though it's hard to think where off the top of my head. Let's compare: Roy Jenkins – twice Home Secretary, once Chancellor of the Exchequer, a man on whose watch homosexuality was decriminalised, abortion was legalised, capital punishment was abolished and archaic divorce laws were reformed; Chuka Umunna – Shadow Business Secretary...and...er...well, that's it. And yet, at the press conference held to announce the resignation of seven Labour MPs this morning, Umunna did his best to remix the speech Jenkins made at the launch of the SDP in 1981 so that it could become a defining signpost along his own path of vainglory.

When a mere four 'moderate' MPs staged a similar split from a Labour party that had been seized by the hard left thirty-eight years ago, the quartet consisted of the aforementioned Jenkins as well as a former Foreign Secretary (David Owen), a former Education Secretary (Shirley Williams), and a former Transport Secretary (Bill Rodgers). Rodgers was perhaps the only member of the quartet whose public service didn't quite resonate with the heavyweight cache of his partners, though seeing today's events on TV made me think

11

of legendary US rock critic Lester Bang's response to the question, 'Are Slade the new Beatles?' – to which he had replied, 'Sure; they're all Ringo.' What we witnessed today was seven Ringos who hadn't even formulated the concept of an actual political party, merely a 'group'. The Gang of Seven, perhaps.

Various reasons were served-up as motives for the split, varying from individual to individual. The case of Luciana Berger (Liverpool Wavertree) seemed the most understandable, subject as she has been over the past five years to unpleasant anti-Semitic abuse that the leadership of the Labour Party appears either incapable – or unwilling – to get an effective grip on. Her resignation was perhaps the most anticipated and probably would have happened with or without the simultaneous walk-out of six fellow Labour MPs. But while dissatisfaction with the direction of the party has been brewing amongst those who graduated from the Blair academy ever since Corbyn took control in 2015, the shadow of Brexit hangs over the whole affair like the 'I'd give it ten minutes if I were you' post-toilet warning of an unwelcome houseguest.

Three or four Tory MPs are currently facing threats of de-selection thanks to their Brexit stance and it's not beyond the realm of possibility to picture them joining their ideological cohorts who have just exited Labour; and, somewhat predictably, the Mr Barrowclough of British politics, Vince 'I sold the Royal Mail' Cable has offered the hand of friendship to the 'Independent Group', echoing as they seem to do his own perspective on Brexit. Whether or not this means all three strands will coalesce into a new third party remains to be seen, but – a bit like Jacob Rees-Mogg's melodramatic misfire re Theresa May's leadership last year – the timing of this decision could well prove to be somewhat ill.

One of the criticisms levelled at Jenkins & co in 1981 was that they should have remained in the Labour Party and engaged in a battle that could have seen them eventually wrestle control from Foot and Benn; their exit was viewed in some quarters as a cowardly cop-out, being all-too aware that the structure of the British political system meant their Social Democratic experiment was destined to ensure a further two Election successes for Mrs Thatcher. The last time a third party was able to command more than 100 seats in Parliament was way back in 1923, and since then the role of a third party has essentially been to prop up the winners, most notably in 2010. At the moment, this Independent Group haven't even got to the stage where they can call themselves a party, which makes their little collective more reminiscent of an even older Parliamentary model, one that stretches all the way back to the eighteenth century, when Whigs and Tories were ideological groupings at Westminster rather than organised political parties as we would recognise them today.

It's hard not to be cynical towards the motives of Umunna in particular. He quickly threw his hat in the ring following Ed Miliband's resignation as Labour leader after the 2015 General Election defeat and withdrew it just as quickly, suggesting he lacked the bottle to push himself forward as a potential Prime Minister when he belatedly realised the level of scrutiny he'd be subjected to. Since his hissy-fit departure from the frontbench in the wake of Corbyn's 2015 election as Labour leader, his evident irritation with being shoved to the margins of Labour has rankled with his ego, something that's been on constant display during his regular television appearances over the last couple of years. He's also had to stand back and watch his own elitist outlook take battering after battering across the Continent, yet his denial over precisely how out of touch he is with the prevailing European trend echoes his guru Tony's equally deluded sermons on the subject of Brexit. The world has moved on, but these people simply will not accept they are now standing on the wrong side of history.

Along with his kindred spirit in the blue half of the Commons, Anna Soubry, Chuka Umunna has been prominent in doing his utmost to block Brexit progress, emerging as one of the leading cheerleaders of the 'You plebs didn't understand what you were voting for' mindset. In Chuka's world, the Third Way approach that worked in the 90s is still relevant, whereas most of the electorate see it as meaningless an approach to today's problems as the Gold Standard or any other archaic political foundation stone upon which to build a system of governance. Few are arguing that a satisfactory successor has taken hold of this century; so far, there seem to be a series of competing ideologies, all of which are fighting to make themselves heard without any emerging as a distinct frontrunner. Such a climate is commonplace in the prelude to war, though that's hardly a comforting thought.

All seven members of the Independent Group have fairly secure majorities from the last General Election, so it's no wonder they're reluctant to call on their constituents to endorse their walk-out via a series of potentially fascinating by-elections. Many hail from Leave constituencies, which (considering their shared stance on Brexit) is no doubt another factor in hesitating to put it to the people – unless it's a second Referendum, of course; that's different. Oh, well. We'll see what happens in the days and weeks to come. At least if they've achieved anything, they've prompted me back into action; and that's an achievement in itself.

I guess they really do believe we're stupid. True, if one were to gauge the IQ of the masses by, say, monitoring click-bait and being unsurprisingly struck by the insensible numbers who find half-naked synth-faced freaks on red carpets inexplicably interesting, it'd be hard not to come away concluding that we *are* stupid. But the powers-that-be couldn't regard us as less retarded than they already do even if each and every one of us signed-up to worship at the altar of the Kardashians.

Jeremy Corbyn has indicated it will now be official Labour Party policy to back an amendment for a second EU Referendum if MPs vote down its plans for an alternative to Theresa May's dead Brexit duck. This uncannily timely move, following a week in which nine MPs left the party – eight of them lining up alongside a trio of renegade Tories – is a blatantly opportunistic tactic when Brexit was the driving force that spawned the Independent Group and Corbyn badly needs to shift the spotlight away from anti-Semitism accusations. Desperate to stem the haemorrhaging of more MPs, Jezza – or those pulling his strings – has belatedly nailed his colours to the Remoaner mast, appeasing the dominant Remain faction that has yet to quit the party and sticking two fingers up at the sizeable amount of Labour constituencies that voted Leave. Emily (Lady Nugee) Thornberry could barely contain her excitement, though we already know what she thinks of the plebs anyway.

Having apparently abandoned tiresome demands for a General Election it still probably wouldn't win, Labour is now hedging its bets on the Second Referendum factor as a means of improving its pitiful position in the polls. It's probably not a wild, unrealistic assumption that most of the fresh recruits to the party who (so we were told) joined in their millions during the height of Jezza-mania a couple of years ago are in favour of a Second Referendum; these are no doubt the Bright Young Things that Polly Toynbee hopes will slip cyanide into the cocoa of the demented elderly racists and xenophobes who voted Leave. In the same way that the leading three sci-fi franchises – 'Star Trek', 'Star Wars' and 'Doctor Who' – have alienated their loyal hardcore audiences to chase the Woke vote, with Labour it now seems to be a case of sod the constituents that have supported the party through many a lean decade.

Just as well things aren't as bad on the blue side of the Commons, eh? Er...well, with Theresa May's endless fruitless trips to Brussels making her look more and more like a rejected suitor who still insists on serenading the object of her affection even when that object has repeatedly told her to f*** off, the Cabinet is once more doing whatever the hell it likes while the cat's away. When it comes to exercising effective authority, the Prime Minister is akin to a supply teacher fresh out of training college, thrown in at the deep end with a classroom full of surly Easter-leavers exploiting her timidity; it would appear the suspension of collective responsibility that Cameron introduced for the EU Referendum in 2016 has now become standard practice.

In the wake of the three amigos' defection, half-a-dozen members of the Cabinet have flexed their muscles and delivered yet another raspberry in the direction of May's 'authority', threatening mass resignations if the Prime Minister doesn't extend the Article 50 deadline and rule out No Deal. Has there ever been a PM with such a staggering lack of control over her own Ministers? For those of us who can recall the clout that Blair or Thatcher wielded, it really is a remarkable situation to witness. Of course, with May having declared she won't fight the next General Election as Conservative Party leader, there's clearly jostling for future leadership going on, though one suspects there's something a little more personal in Amber Rudd's contribution. Maybe it still rankles that she lost her job and carried the can for the Windrush scandal when most of the damage had been done by her predecessor at the Home Office – though Rudd would do well to remember she retained her seat at Hastings and Rye by a mere 346 votes in 2017, making the foundations upon which to build a bid for No.10 decidedly shaky.

Corbyn's Second Referendum announcement, the Remainer revolt in the Cabinet, and the Independent Group – all symptoms of the same thing that has been going on at Westminster for the past two-and-a-half years; and the reason this issue is still dragging its rotting carcass across the front page of everyone's lives in 2019 – indeed the reason Parliament has made such a God-awful bloody mess of the whole issue – appears obvious. Parliament on the whole does not want what the majority of British people voted for and is determined to prevent it from happening. If it achieves this aim, God knows what will happen the next time the electorate has an opportunity to intervene; it would be extremely unwise for our elected representatives to imagine their actions will not have serious repercussions both for them and for the widening fault-lines running through society.

As stated in a previous post, I voted Remain in 2016 and have subsequently altered my opinion on the subject solely as a consequence of my disgust with the blatant disregard of democracy that has been taking place at Westminster ever since. Most of the prominent MPs who retained their seats at the last General Election were elected on the basis they would honour, respect and (if in government) implement the

Referendum result. They did so to a man and – surprise, surprise – they lied. Their real intention seems to have been to prevent Brexit from happening, and they're more determined than ever to do so as we edge closer to D-Day. It's no use now claiming that a Second Referendum is the only solution to breaking the deadlock. Why is there a deadlock? Because they have engineered it in order to bring about their hoped-for solution.

You can't always get what you want, as someone once said. I might have preferred the UK to remain in the EU in 2016, but I accepted the result, as one does – or *should* do. The people that voted Leave are not to blame for the current crisis; MPs are. And, like the teenager whose response to a parental edict to tidy their bedroom is to keep repeating 'I'll do it in a minute' in the hope they won't have to, MPs seem to believe if they delay the process indefinitely the public will get so sick of the whole business that they'll eventually stop caring and will accept the betrayal with a resigned shrug of the shoulders. At this rate, the whole sorry saga seems set to make *Jarndyce v Jarndyce* resemble the career duration of an X-Factor winner.

STARMER CHAMELEON
2 March 2019

I've always found 'The Week in Westminster' to be one of the more engaging political bastions of Radio 4; the programme being broadcast on a Saturday morning enables it to benefit from the breathing space denied the likes of 'Today' or 'The World at One', which are both designed to cater for the gut (and knee-jerk) reaction in the immediate aftermath of events. A gap of seven days rather than seven minutes certainly gives rise to a preferable perspective, particularly in our instant age, when a comment is required on the spot and (often) without the facts. MPs of all the major parties are usually represented, as are MPs of old, many of whom have invaluable hindsight that even elevation to the ermine slippers of the Lords hasn't entirely blunted.

I had to laugh at the latest instalment, however, when the merits of Labour's Shadow Brexit Secretary were being discussed – and some of the conclusions reached were so worryingly ludicrous that laughter seemed the only tonic. Sir Keir Starmer was seriously touted as a future Labour leader in the event of Jezza losing the next General Election. For those whose memories of this man stretch back to his insidious activities as Director of Public Prosecutions, this isn't necessarily a welcome solution to the monopoly of the party by the hard left. Moreover, that a man so lacking in charisma and one in possession of an android-like demeanour that is actually quite chilling in its absence of recognisable human qualities could be considered as a Labour leader (and possible Prime Minister in the process) is yet another cause for concern in a time of many.

In order to justify the terrible pun in the title of this post, I suppose I could say the second most notable Keir in the history of the Labour Party has held onto his frontbench seat by effortlessly blending in to the Corbyn worldview when many of his true ideological allies in the party stormed off not long after Jezza's election. Starmer has been able to do so because he appears to be so devoid of personality that few have noticed he doesn't quite fit the Socialist suit that is otherwise a prerequisite for membership of Team Corbyn. He also confirmed long-held suspicions this week by eagerly embracing the Second Referendum option, promoting the People's Vote as official Labour policy, a move that places him on the same wavelength as the Independent Group, meaning the Starmer Chameleon now has a foot in two

Westminster camps, utterly befitting a man who appears to be a blank canvas that anyone can draw a cock and balls on.

Starmer's background is in Law; he qualified as a barrister in 1987 and became a QC five years later. Within a decade, he was named as the DPP (and therefore head of the CPS) following the retirement of Sir Ken Macdonald. Starmer courted controversy just two years into the job when he announced the police officer Simon Harwood would not be prosecuted in relation to the death of London newsvendor Ian Tomlinson, despite video evidence of Harwood striking Tomlinson on the leg with his baton and then pushing him onto the pavement, allegedly mistaking him for an unlikely G-20 Summit protestor in 2009. The unprovoked assault led to Tomlinson collapsing and dying moments later. However, the initial CPS decision was later reversed and Harwood was tried for manslaughter in 2012, found not guilty.

On Starmer's watch, the CPS also pursued a case against Paul Chambers in the so-called 'Twitter Joke Trial', following Chambers' frustrated tweet in 2010 after a flight he had booked was cancelled due to bad weather and he jokingly threatened to blow Robin Hood Airport 'sky high'. The farcical legal action became something of a *cause célèbre* for notable comedy figures such as Stephen Fry and Al Murray. Chambers eventually had his conviction quashed in 2012, though rumours emerged that the CPS were prepared to drop the case until Starmer intervened and overruled them; Paul Chambers' MP at the time, Louise Mensch, called for an investigation into Starmer's behaviour by a Commons committee, though blame for the decision to pursue the case was laid at the door of the crown court and Starmer evaded scrutiny.

Starmer's most damaging legacy as DPP, however, was to vigorously push through the 'victim's law', a legal code of practice especially aimed at tipping the balance in favour of complainants in cases relating to sexual abuse. As a highly vocal promoter of Operation Yewtree at the hysterical height of the celebrity witch-hunt in the wake of the Jimmy Savile 'revelations', Starmer's proposals were to seriously undermine the rights of defendants in such cases, creating the corrosive climate whereby police forces would not only instantly assume any allegation of a sexual nature to be 'credible and true' (AKA 'I Believe Her'), but would co-operate with the CPS drive to improve stats on rape convictions by deliberately withholding vital evidence from the defence in order to secure a guilty verdict.

Establishing the comfort blanket of video evidence exclusively for the complainant as the norm and thus only exposing the accused to the lion's den of the courtroom, Starmer's rejection of the traditional fair fight has given the green light to every vindictive fantasist and serial accuser ever since. One wonders how many innocent men (and their families) have suffered the trauma of an extended police investigation without even reaching court or are actually languishing behind bars as a consequence of Starmer's seal of approval on dispensing with the age-old 'innocent until proven guilty' Golden Thread of British justice. I'm sure they'd all be ecstatic at the prospect of Starmer one day being the leader of their country.

Starmer had advised the Labour opposition on his proposals in the hope the party would return to government in 2015; it didn't, but Starmer himself joined the party's ranks at Westminster after winning the seat of Holborn and St Pancras at that year's General Election. The shit sorcerer had already handed the reins of power at the CPS to his awful apprentice

Alison Saunders, who built on Starmer's blueprint by steering the reputation of the Law to such a calamitous low that Sir Keir must have imagined he was well out of it; but even though Saunders too has now vacated the post, she has left behind an almighty bloody mess for which her predecessor must take a great deal of the credit. And this is the man some are touting as a future occupant of No.10. Hah. And we think we've got it bad now.

NO PLACE LIKE HOME
9 March 2019

Blame it on John Craven. Without 'Newsround', I probably wouldn't have been aware of numerous stories that grabbed headlines when I was an otherwise disinterested schoolboy in the mid-70s, ones provoking many questions that began with the prefix 'Mum' or 'Dad'. Alas, poor parents, presented with enquiries re white mercenaries heading for the Dark Continent – how to explain the presence of Brits in the likes of Angola? At that time, I had yet to hear Johnny Rotten's reference, 'is this the MPLA?' due to the BBC's post-Grundy blanket ban of 'Anarchy in the UK', and wouldn't have got it anyway; my babysitters (largely secretaries from my father's firm) professed more of a fondness for The Real Thing. Maybe comparisons back then were made with those who had volunteered for action in the Spanish Civil War forty years previously. Such comparisons emerged anew when Syria exploded into conflict forty years later.

There's a difference, though. British recruits to the International Brigades of the 1930s were mostly motivated by idealistic (if naive) anti-fascist principles, whereas 70s mercenaries were motivated by money, despite attempts to paint them as heroic upholders of White Africa at a time when minority colonials were engaged in an increasingly desperate

22

and doomed struggle to retain control over the natives and their Marxist leanings. Come the Arab Spring aftermath and the turmoil it gave birth to in Syria, however, religion reared its ugly head as the prime motivator and did so via newfangled methods of recruitment courtesy of the inter-web thingy.

It's interesting in a week that saw sympathy for professional pissers on yet another famous grave – those whose bladders were emptied for the voyeuristic delectation of TV viewers prepared to accept their wobbly testimony against a dead man as Gospel (yes, we've been here before) – that concepts of innocent children groomed by knowing elders didn't extend to those rendered stateless by their misplaced embrace of a nihilistic philosophy that even racism sniffer-dogs like Lammy and Abbott are hard-pressed to present as one more legacy of Evil White Men. Yesterday, it was confirmed that the baby born to 'ISIS Bride' Shamima Begum has died in the same refugee camp that his short, miserable life began in just three weeks ago.

It must be difficult for Guardian readers to fall back on favoured accusations when the blood of this unfortunate British subject is seemingly on the hands of a Home Secretary who inconveniently happens to be a Muslim. The decision of Sajid Javid to strip the baby's mother of her citizenship has been seen by some as a cynical, populist move in a bid for the Tory leadership during the run-up to Theresa May's imminent exit, whereas others have viewed it as another example of the Home Secretary's 'Coconut' tendencies. Whichever perspective one takes, however, the refusal to retrieve Shamima Begum and her newborn from the Syrian hellhole they were discovered in by the war correspondent for the Times has now taken a tragic turn with this latest announcement.

The recruitment of deluded British Muslims to the ISIS cause in Syria four or five years back was facilitated by the same call-to-romantic-arms previously utilised by old-school paramilitary outfits such as the IRA. In the States, armchair Irish Republicans who had never set foot in the Emerald Isle gleefully contributed to the begging bowls passed around Boston bars, having being seduced by deep-rooted sentimental attachment to inherited Irishness; but (luckily for those funding 'the revolution') flying to Belfast to participate in person wasn't deemed necessary. Comparisons with Brits who made the journey to Spain eighty years ago are more prescient in the case of Syria, though few of those 30s idealists rushed to join the fascist cause; the prevailing aim was to *fight* fascism. In contrast, home-grown ISIS recruits were knowingly signing-up to a blatantly barbaric death cult that had never shied away from publicising its methods of madness; nobody, however young, naive or gullible, could have responded to the ISIS cry for help utterly ignorant of what it would ultimately entail. Shamima Begum showed herself to be a resourceful young woman far from clueless when she embarked on her backpacking gap-year with a difference, despite being legally defined as a child. She's still only just 19, yet is now stateless, and has three dead babies to her name. At least she's one 19-year-old who can't blame Brexit for 'stealing her future'.

In the recent blitz of media coverage afforded this articulate adolescent since her discovery, the absence of remorse in her account of her Jihadi holiday convinced many that bringing her back would sow seeds of future atrocities on home soil. Had she sought public redemption by shedding tears and pleading for forgiveness in the manner of a disgraced celebrity coached by Max Clifford before the late PR guru was hoisted by his own petard, perhaps the assertion that she poses no threat to the UK would have sealed her return; post-

Diana, few emotional gestures provoke a sympathetic response in Brits more than the waterworks. Instead, like a disability claimant failing an ATOS assessment, Begum forgot to play the victim and has therefore faced the harshest consequences.

The complicated case of Shamima Begum and what to do with her has presented politicians with many problems, and in the process has exposed some double standards in the definition of children. If, rather than volunteering for Holy War service, Begum had been involved in a sexual relationship with her teacher when weeks away from her 16th birthday, she would have been viewed as an innocent, blameless victim of grooming and regarded as unable to distinguish between consent and rape. Yet, the fact she made her way to join ISIS in Syria as a 15-year-old by cannily using her older sister's passport appears to negate the blameless innocence that would have applied in the aforementioned other circumstances. Yes, the facts suggest she knowingly endorsed the philosophy of an organisation committed to eradicating western civilisation – one responsible for the deaths of many of Begum's countrymen and women; but surely the indoctrination she received presumably online and (possibly) within her own community is a classic case of grooming as so severely defined in other areas of the law?

Blair's disastrous faith schools policy and the willingness of police and politicians to leave 'them' to their own devices when it comes to education and designs for life for fear of being labelled racist or Islamophobic has helped engineer the situation that allows some Muslim communities to be effectively governed in the style of Mafiosi Sicily or the East End during the reign of the Krays. It has enabled hate preachers to have a platform or underage white girls to be repeatedly abused by gangs or a 15-year-old Muslim schoolgirl to voluntarily put herself in one of the most dangerous environments on the planet. Sadly, the multicultural fault-lines run much deeper than one person stripped of her nationality or one freshly buried baby.

EXTENDED PLAY
16 March 2019

What a voice. The rich, booming baritone of Attorney General Geoffrey Cox resonated in every crumbling crevice of the Commons this week, conveying the kind of old-school aural authority our ears have rarely been massaged by since it was rendered unfashionable. At one time, a voice like that would have read the news headlines on Radio 4 or at the very least delivered the football results with sonorous sonic expertise. Quite a contrast with the fingernails-on-a-blackboard croak of Our Glorious Leader; even before she lost it, Theresa May's voice was always a reedy, hectoring whine of a sort that conveys no authority at all – which is pretty fitting because she has none.

The members of her Cabinet piss all over the naughty step on a daily basis; they're like kids running riot in some grotty family featured on a Channel 4 documentary probably called 'Unruly Britain' or something of that nature. And like children with a weak, compliant parent incapable of administering any form of discipline, they know they can get away with murder. They can vote against their own government or publicly abstain from voting at all, despite the neutered entreaties of the whips. It must be great being a member of the Cabinet at the moment. Mind you, you don't need to be in the Cabinet to take the piss out of the PM to her face.

When the Maybot tried to serve up her already-rejected motorway service-station meal to Parliament for a second time, adding a sprig of Irish parsley fooled nobody and she received another chorus-line of moonies for her efforts. Undeterred, she'll probably emerge from the kitchen with the same dish next week and plonk it back on the table. It may give her diners indigestion, but she'll remind them it's better than no dinner at all, which is the only other option available to them.

Delaying D-Day may have been voted for this week, but apparently this typical tactic of a Parliament overwhelmingly opposed to the Referendum result is still dependent on the approval of all EU colonies – sorry, *member states* – so actual Brexit remains the default outcome on March 29. It would seem, however, that the PM will snatch a sorry victory from the jaws of defeat with such a sword hanging over Westminster. A rotten deal twice rejected by massive majorities could well pass third time round because May has consistently stuck her fingers in her ears when anyone has suggested anything else. She has ground down dissenting voices by refusing to budge as the minutes have continued to tick away.

In some respects, it's a remarkable achievement on her part, though hardly one worthy of celebration. She'll finally persuade all the knockers within her shambles of a party to vote her way even though they know her offer is shit; but the persistent propaganda of Project Fear has scared so many that they'll no doubt fall into line in the end; and she'll genuinely believe she's led the nation out of the dark. It's like settling for a loveless marriage because it's preferable to being a sad singleton. Promoters of the so-called 'People's Vote' have advocated a similar absence of choice with the proposed

Second Referendum options of a) Remain or b) May's deal, AKA a) Remain or b) Diet Remain.

As the PM offers a fresh pair of Brussels handcuffs rather than the key to the ones we're already wearing, one of her more notorious predecessors cosies up with Macron behind closed doors, and the Remain righteousness of the media mafia mirrors the smug smile of a Guardian columnist's profile picture; social media sneering and jeering at a pro-Leave protest march setting off on the long road from Sunderland to Westminster sums up a kind of despondent capitulation to the way we were and will always be. Everything appears to have changed, but when the dust eventually settles, maybe nothing will have after all.

Two and-a-half years ago, I guess I was one of them, but it still amazes me how many smart, intelligent people who rarely suffer fools gladly are content to defend a privileged coalition whose policies were responsible for the 2008 crash and who have imposed a decade of austerity upon everyone outside of their cosseted bubble whilst either outsourcing or effectively abolishing public services the majority depend on. But when the alternative is portrayed as some post-apocalyptic far-right racist state run by Old Etonians and policed by gammons, I suppose it's no wonder, really. And those whose laurels must stink due to being sat on for so long continue to pedal the favoured narrative as long as they're listened to; I don't imagine comfortable comedians whose last funny joke was laughed at sometime in the mid-90s are that concerned with towns in the North East or Midlands that mean no more to them than obscure names on a pools coupon.

There are probably still a few out there who would like to see Mr Blair tried as a war criminal; but if any former PM deserves a public flogging, it's that absentee ex-resident of

No.10 who plunged us into this bloody mess, Mr Cameron. I heard his swift resignation described as 'honourable' this week, in the context of his successor's refusal to fall on her sword; but heading for his caravan barely a year after winning a General Election and leaving the nation to fend for itself like an abandoned puppy seems pretty criminal to me. Maybe he sees us as leftover volunteers for his Big Society project and figured we all had unused brooms knocking about.

Gallows humour, satire and sarcasm serve as a way of enduring this daily grind. I used to be an optimistic romantic, whereas now I'm a hard, cynical c*** without an iota of love left in me, so I need to employ some coping mechanism. I always thought I was a man out of time, but it would appear I'm very much a man *of* my time. Life is full of surprises, but it could be a hell of a lot worse; we realised that on Friday. Back for more next week, no doubt.

THE SHOW THAT NEVER ENDS
30 March 2019

And there was me expecting Friday's 'Newsnight' to come live from the white cliffs of Dover, whereupon Jacob Rees-Mogg, Boris, Nigel and Tommy Robinson were scheduled to link arms at 11.00pm and treat us all to a rousing chorus of 'Jerusalem'. It didn't happen. I should imagine our lords and masters across the Channel were poised to give us *nul points* in the event, but there's always 12 April. Don't bank on it. Not tweaked quite enough and still not convincing enough for 344 dishonourable members, it was third time unlucky for Mrs May's deal earlier in the day and, after a week in which Parliament 'took control' from the executive only to prove itself just as inept, the day that should have been *the* day ended in one more damp squib.

Theresa May's tactic of dragging this out till the last minute so that the only alternative to her deal is no deal has proven to be as disastrous as all her other tactics. But is anyone really surprised anymore? Few fell for her crass offer of throwing money at deprived communities 'oop north'; few fell for the carrot of knighthoods and peerages; and few fell for her announcement that she'd quit if her withdrawal agreement passed. Yes, even the ultimate sacrifice that most in her party crave failed to bring in the required numbers. The PM has tried to wheel and deal, but she's no Harold Wilson.

According to some reports, May is going to try again next week; if it fails, she'll probably give it another go the week after...and the week after that...and on and on and on until we all take the route recommended by the Reverend Jim Jones. Our Glorious Leader doesn't yet seem to have realised she's not running an administration with a vast majority, one that gives her carte blanche to do what the hell she likes without having to acknowledge any other views in her divided house. I suspect some have attempted to point that out to her, but I've a feeling she probably stuck her fingers in her ears and went 'Blaah blaah blaah blaah.' I don't believe a second referendum will resolve this bloody mess, nor do I believe a General Election will; but at the moment, the latter option seems absolutely essential, if only as a political laxative to end Westminster's constipation and prompt a much-needed evacuation.

I became conscious and aware of the institution of Parliament and the office of Prime Minister perhaps around the time of the two 1974 Elections; kids ask questions, especially when they get a day off school and it's not a Bank Holiday. Therefore, I've lived through quite a few different Governments of different colours over the last 40-odd years and I've occasionally done my bit at the polling station. But I can honestly say this staggering shambles that keeps defying the odds by outdoing itself is unprecedented in my lifetime. It simply cannot go on for much longer in its current incarnation, and neither can the Conservative Party with a leader capable of giving IDS a run for his money as its worst ever.

But then what? Looking at the prospective replacements for May feels like swiping through the world's worst dating app, whereas Corbyn's frontbench is about as appetising as the 'reduced' goods past their sell-by date on a supermarket shelf. Could any of them really do any better? And even if one takes the egos of the worst offenders into account, what madman or woman would really relish stepping into May's hideous shoes right now? Theresa May won't be packing up the nation's troubles in an old kit bag when she exits Downing Street; they'll all still be here when she's gone. A General Election won't magically wave them away, but I suppose it might possibly serve as a *de facto* referendum in terms of the electorate having their say on how their elected representatives have handled things since the last time the hustings were active. It's hard to see an imminent General Election as anything else at this moment in time, despite the backlog of other pressing issues that are gathering dust and languishing in a criminal state of neglect.

A friend of mine recently spoke of how he had gradually reduced the amount of time he spends inhabiting the parallel universe of social media and feels all the better for it. Indeed, the more hours in a day one spends within the realms of that facsimile reality, the more one loses touch with the fact that its daily howl barely registers beyond the borders of cyberspace. 'Are trans-women real women?' isn't necessarily the question on the lips of people juggling limited finances and deciding which bill takes priority this month; perhaps those with the luxury of debating trivialities regard them with such importance because they're not plagued with moribund concerns. The thought that identity politics mean anything to those outside of the context social media junkies operate in is laughable. If one were to take Twitter as a microcosm of the real world then Titania McGrath would be Prime Minister.

While the brilliant spoof account of Titania McGrath satirises detachment via inherited privilege and/or bourgeois metropolitan comfort, one cannot help but see Westminster as a similarly detached bubble – with the significant difference being these living, breathing caricatures *are* affecting the lives of real people. The actual issues that have had a traumatic impact on the lives of those on the other side of that bubble have barely touched those inside it, hence the absence of empathy and absence of conscience when continuing to inflict them upon the rest of the populace or outsourcing them to some useless private company only in it for the profit. Perhaps empathy would be rated a little higher if the eye-opening experiment Matthew Parris took part in for 'World in Action' in the early 80s, living off the minimum benefits his government declared sufficient for living off, was compulsory training for every prospective MP.

The disconnect between elected and electorate that probably dates from the Expenses' Scandal and Hackgate has only been intensified by Brexit, but the deliberate policy of delaying tactics which all colours have been guilty of seems to demonstrate the political class has learnt nothing from the last ten years. Events of the past week-and-a-bit have done little to alter my opinion of our elected representatives or their celebrity cheerleaders. Much is made of the ERG school of rich Brexiteer; but what of the loudest voices from the other side? Whether residing in the nicer parts of London, the nicer parts of the Home Counties, or simply wealthy ex-pats, these voices are not unlike those of the Hollywood-based Scots that the SNP flew over for the 2014 Independence Referendum, before swiftly depositing them back on Californian soil after the vote so they could avoid paying backdated UK tax. Weariness with endless lectures from wealthy chaps is something both sides of this divide share; but at least it means we've got something in common. Maybe we should use it to our advantage.

GAVIN IN STASIS
2 May 2019

I must admit, it is hard to attribute anything approaching a heroic act to a member of Theresa May's Cabinet; one cannot avoid being suspicious and seeing self-promotion as the motivation behind every move made in public. 'Will it help make me look good before the electorate and boost my impending leadership bid if I'm photographed alongside an autistic adolescent in pigtails who has somehow become the poster-girl for climate change?' and so on. It's so difficult not to be cynical about politicians today that even when one of them might actually have done something for purely selfless reasons, crediting them with it is a tough call tinged with suspicious reservations.

The sacking of Defence Secretary Gavin Williamson has been officially justified because he was named as the source of the leak surrounding the National Security Council's discussion over the Chinese Government's telecommunications wing, Huawei, being invited to get its feet under the UK's online table. Williamson denies this rather serious allegation whilst Jeremy Hunt has become the latest Minister to undermine the PM's (non) authority by suggesting a police investigation wouldn't be out of the question, contradicting Mrs May's own decision not to pursue the matter beyond firing Williamson. If the ex-Defence Secretary *is* guilty, why did he do it when he must have realised the potential damage it could do to his political ambitions? Could it actually have been that extremely rare Westminster beast, a case of conscience over career?

Let's face it, Gavin Williamson is not an easy man to warm to; then again, name me a member of the Cabinet who is. I know we're all born with the face God gave us, but Williamson's ego does seem to be etched on his smug countenance; I may be doing him a disservice, but to me he has the arrogant air of an office-worker celebrating promotion with a trip to a lap-dancing bar, where he probably waves a wad in a young lady's face in expectation of a blowjob. His attempts to cultivate a Mandelson-like 'Dark Arts' image have been cringeworthy from the off. From his pet tarantula to his 'ooh, you're hard' boast that he had 'made' Theresa May and could therefore just as easily 'break' her, Williamson's role as the mastermind behind May's leadership election and then organising the bribery of the DUP gave rise to his reputation as Kingmaker, and he appeared to be a man May couldn't manage without – until now.

The Tory Chair of the Defence Select Committee, Dr Julian Lewis, was one Williamson ally speaking up for the deposed Minister last night. Dr Lewis pointed out that Williamson wasn't the only member of the Cabinet to express reservations over the wisdom of awarding contracts to corporations answerable to a Communist regime not averse to keeping tabs on its citizens. Unsurprisingly for someone who has enthusiastically embraced any form of internet snooping since her days as Home Secretary, the PM was in favour of allowing Huawei to play a part in this country's 5G network – something no other western leader has even contemplated; by all accounts, Williamson was appalled by this development and appears to have risked his role in Government (and possible rise all the way to the top job) by passing on his concerns to Fleet Street.

I would hesitate to call the information leaked a 'sensitive state secret'; it appears to be more a case of where the information was leaked *from* – a body established during Cameron's tenure, somewhere Ministers and officials could discuss clandestine topics free from the public gaze; and what could be more clandestine than offering the Chinese a chance to buy into Britain's internet system? No wonder they wanted that one kept under wraps. But, as Julian Lewis rightly stated, the nature of the information Gavin Williamson is alleged to have leaked hardly places him in the same treasonous league as Kim Philby or George Blake. What Williamson has done – if indeed, he has done it – is to spill the beans on just how shamelessly willing our senior elected representatives are to flog anything to the highest bidder, free from any principles or sense of scruples; as long as they can make a mint from outsourcing, they'll do it. Just look at who replaced ATOS with the contract for the notorious DWP disability assessments – an equally loathsome US corporation short on sympathy for the ill and infirm called Maximus; and the less said about Grayling's ferry fiasco, the better. Should ISIS put in a bid to run all primary schools in England and Wales, they'd probably be in with a shot if their bid was juicy enough.

Williamson's promotion from Chief Whip to Defence Secretary seemed to begin the process of his gradual detachment from the PM's inner circle, especially when he became a tad prone to the odd gaffe and earned the nickname of 'Private Pike' among some of his less generous colleagues. If he was responsible for the NSC leak, it's hard to see what he had to gain from his actions being uncovered other than alerting the rest of us to the seriously worrying shit that goes on behind closed doors at Downing Street, as opposed to the silly in-fighting and backstabbing we're used to hearing about. And, if that was what happened, he deserves credit – however begrudgingly we give it him.

Another Tory MP, Adam Holloway, made a wider point in relation to Williamson last night, stating how he believed contemporary politicians just aren't up to it, whatever the challenge presented to them might be. Ministers find themselves in positions of power they simply aren't qualified to do justice to, lacking both leadership skills and any talent beyond generating sufficient hype around them in the manner of a band desperate for a record deal; how else can we explain so many 'name' MPs who have risen without a trace in the past decade? A former military man, Adam Holloway said most of the current Cabinet would be 'very unlikely to rise to the rank of General'; it's certainly hard looking across both benches in the Commons and seeing anyone with the heavyweight clout of a Benn or a Thatcher. Or perhaps past politicians were forged in different ages that deserved different leaders; despite the grimly serious issues facing the country, we appear to have reaped the harvest of the 90s, when style triumphed over substance in all facets of public life.

The fact a figure as friendless as Theresa May can fire someone who was once such a vital ally suggests the embarrassment of this particular leak must have been acute for the Prime Minister, even when one considers the Cabinet Office has shown itself to have the consistency of a sieve over the last couple of years. Williamson's dramatic dismissal and possible breach of the Official Secrets Act may well be as 'unprecedented' as media folk kept claiming yesterday, but the leak is merely emblematic of a chaotic Cabinet environment with a grasp of authority reminiscent of St Trinian's. The timing of this latest unwelcome headline from the PM's perspective, on the very eve of possible obliteration in the local elections, suggests Williamson's alleged crime is a little more serious than some that have resulted in sackings of late; but yet another enemy on the backbenches could be just one more nail in the Maybot coffin. Not all bad news, then.

REAP THE WILD WIND
12 May 2019

It pays to flick through past posts if approaching a topic I've written about on previous occasions, if only to avoid repetition. Past posts can also be handy ways of assessing not necessarily predictions, but attempts at guessing where we might go next. Well, few knew before and fewer still know now – that much is true today. The talk at the end of last year and the start of this was anticipating a move by restless centrist politicians from both left and right meeting in the middle to form their own SDP-like breakaway party that would allegedly appeal to moderates alienated by the warring factions on either side of the Brexit barricade. That appeared to be the only change on the cards; and though it eventually happened, any new party dependent on oily Umunna and sour-faced Soubry is facing far more of an uphill challenge than the one formed by Jenkins, Owens, Williams and Rodgers almost 40 years ago.

What began as 'TIG' and has now been rebranded Change UK isn't exactly taking the country by storm. Whereas the SDP peaked at a 50% poll rating in the autumn of 1981 (less than a year after its formation), the apathy greeting Change UK is a consequence of the conceit of its founders. All are second division strikers, with not one of them having scored one of the great offices of state; but their high opinion of themselves and belief that their outdated approach remains relevant has blinded them to a sea-change in the public mood that is seeing an even newer party steal the headlines and soar way ahead of them in the polls. The Change UK attitude is to dismiss Nigel Farage's Brexit Party as a right-wing rest-home for bonkers old Tories and ex-UKIP fruitcakes; their smug arrogance in dismissing something they should be taking very seriously will be their undoing, but will they listen? What do you think?

The BBC's archaic attempts at impartiality saw last Friday's scheduled edition of 'Have I Got News For You' pulled at the last minute because one of the guest panellists was Change UK's Heidi Allen. The reason given for this abrupt, eleventh hour cancellation was Allen representing a party intending to participate in the upcoming European Elections, which seems strange; Britain's late entry into the contest was already known on the day the programme was recorded; could not another guest have been chosen? After all, a tub of lard once famously deputised for Roy Hattersley on the show a few years ago. The BBC has a history of panicking when politics risks being treated lightly – infamously axing 'That Was The Week That Was' at the end of 1963, when a General Election was imminent – and is terrified of being seen as favouring one political party over the other, despite its pro-Remain stance being pretty indisputable.

Then again, the BBC (as with all London-centric mainstream media outlets) belongs to the same exclusive gentleman's club as the Westminster set, burying its head in the same sand and pissing in the same pot. Ignoring something in the hope it will simply go away is not good enough at this moment in history. That's precisely what the two major parties have been guilty of for far too long. In 2017, the Conservatives and Labour enjoyed the largest share of the vote the two major parties had managed since 1970, seemingly ending the fragmented era of fringe parties stealing their seats. Now, less than two years on from the last General Election, their failure to honour the 2016 Referendum result (not to mention deliberate efforts at outright prevention) has seen their hard-fought recovery utterly trashed; they've blown it, quite possibly for good.

A new poll published in the Sunday Telegraph puts the Brexit Party one point ahead of the Tories; the poll, by ComRes, is taking a hypothetical survey in the event of a snap General Election, but the findings should shake even the most blinkered, deluded Tories who still cling to the fallacy that Theresa May's repeatedly rejected deal is the only way out of this impasse. The PM herself has told the 1922 Committee she'll finally walk the plank if her deal passes when she drags it before the Commons one more time – the same promise she made last time it faced the firing squad; it didn't work then and it won't work now.

The catastrophic recent local election results from the Conservative perspective – losing over a thousand councillors – saw most of those seats go to the Lib Dems and the Greens; those two claimed they were on the side of the electoral angels in the wake of the results, but there were a record number of spoiled ballot papers in the absence of any Leave candidates. It's a bit like justifying the questionable appointment of Ole Gunnar Solskjaer as permanent Manchester Utd manager on the strength of his results as caretaker, when the team had an easy run of winnable fixtures against lower opposition. They ended the season by losing at home to relegated Cardiff.

If the Tories should be on red alert following the findings of the poll in the Sunday Telegraph – and those of a similar poll by Opinium – Labour have no cause for complacency either.

The pressure by the membership to adopt the Second Referendum route whilst traditional Labour voters in the diehard northern and midlands heartlands remain Leave-inclined has left poor old Jezza looking more at sea and less in control of the party's destiny than ever before. And if the future looks bleak when one contemplates the likely contenders to succeed Mrs May, there's no less despair when one thinks of Tom Watson or Keir Starmer seizing the Corbyn crown. Take two weak leaders surrounded by mediocre wannabes, add a shameful determination to overturn a democratic mandate, throw in dismissive contempt for the concerns of the plebs – and you have a recipe for potential disaster.

If one at least tries to take the long view, it's possible to conclude that a single-issue party run by a man adept at generating publicity and more than capable of exploiting widespread disaffection with the political process is one it's difficult to see being relevant beyond its moment, like a particular pair of trousers fashionable for a solitary season. Closer examination would no doubt uncover not much substance beneath the surface and one could argue Farage's response to an admittedly piss-poor grilling from Andrew Marr was to resort to tried-and-trusted Trump-like tactics, crying media bias and avoiding awkward questions. Yet, the Brexit Party has timed its moment to absolute perfection, and as long the big two keep their fingers in their ears, that moment will retain its relevance.

The need for a new party that can – to paraphrase Roy Jenkins – 'break the mould of British politics' and end the century-old Tory and Labour stranglehold has been pressing for a long time; and though Change UK are (in their minds) attempting to do just that in the old-fashioned way, nobody is interested. It's hard not to feel we've moved on from that now. God knows where we've moved on to or where we're going; but I can't help thinking the old-fashioned way is over. And it's over because those who prospered from it fatally failed to detect the people had had enough. You can only push them so far, and then who knows what they'll do? Just ask Monsieur Macron - or maybe one of his distant predecessors, Louis XVI.

MAY DAZE
22 May 2019

I suppose a turd can only be polished so many times before it's worn down into nothing, even if the turd that Theresa May has been polishing for what feels like a lifetime wasn't exactly a prize-winning stool to begin with. You have to hand it to the Prime Minister, though; she keeps polishing away with her duster and can of Mr Sheen, determined the whole country will see its reflection in it sooner or later; trouble is, that turd has only ever shown *her* reflection, which is apt for a woman who is undoubtedly the shittest holder of her office in living memory. Well, if you can't be blunt now, eh?

On Tuesday, just 48 hours away from another anticipated annihilation at the polling station, the chronically deluded Mrs May unveiled her revised strategy for finally getting her useless EU withdrawal deal through Parliament; and she's surpassed herself yet again, alienating everybody she desperately tried to woo with another series of opportunistic promises that will never be delivered and everyone can see through. At times, her behaviour reminds me of a doomed gambler owing a fortune to a mobster that the debt collector knows cannot be paid, offering everything but the kitchen sink in the absence of cash. 'Take the HD TV set – I've only had it six months and it cost a fortune; take my car – it's worth five grand, easily; take my watch, my mother's engagement ring, the shirt off my back...' BANG!

Ironically, Theresa May has at last achieved something that has seemed impossible for the past couple of years: she's actually united the Commons. Unfortunately for her, she's united it in opposition. Labour, the SNP, the DUP, the Lib Dems, the Greens, and the majority of her own party – all united against what must *surely* be the final despairing throw of the dice for this embarrassingly hapless and hopeless Prime Minister. Brexiteers and Remainers alike have turned their noses up at the latest add-ons to the same old deal, the deal that has been rejected so many times that it's hard to remember which occasions promised which bribes. On one of them, she said she'd quit if it got through; on another, she said the magic money tree in the Downing Street garden would sprout a few notes for deprived communities Oop North if it got through; now, she's even stooped so low as offer a vote on a second referendum if it gets through, one more U-turn for the book. And nobody is buying it.

After six futile weeks of beer & sandwiches chinwags with Labour that resulted in bugger all, May has publicly announced Corbyn-flavoured compromises I suspect she tried out behind closed doors – workers' rights, environmental protection, customs union, and (of course) second referendum – yet the response from the Opposition is the same. John McDonnell had a valid point when he compared entering into an agreement with this Government to signing a contract with a company poised to go into administration. Their word is no bond at all because they are on the verge of collapse, and any agreement would be null and void before the ink had even dried. Everyone bar our lame duck leader can see it. She has changed nobody's mind with this week's model; by the evening following yesterday's announcement, not one MP who was opposed to the deal last time round had declared their conversion to the PM's way of thinking and promised to vote differently.

All of this was pretty inevitable, however. The disastrous gamble of the 2017 General Election was evidence enough that Mrs May was out of her depth on a scale unseen since old Turnip Taylor's memorably woeful stint as England manager in the early 90s. The Tories did not like that, but when they had their opportunity to oust May last December, they bottled it; the absence of an outstanding candidate to replace her and perennial fear of Jezza grabbing the keys to No.10 persuaded the party to retain a leader too obstinate and perhaps too stupid to realise its decision was not motivated by any faith in her ability to get the job done. Most of this could have been prevented, but the Conservative Party is now paying the price for its failure to show May the door.

The Ghost of Referendums Past in the shape of Mr Milkshake himself has returned to haunt the Tories and send them plummeting to the bottom of virtually every poll published over the last month or so; May had already alienated the party's blue-rinsed backbone with certain polices outlined in the 2017 manifesto, but diehard Tory voters are now abandoning their traditional voting preferences handed down like family heirlooms and are flocking in their droves to a party that wouldn't need to exist had Mrs May and her unruly underlings honoured the Referendum result as they told us they would two years ago. Should Theresa May's pitiful premiership ever lay claim to a 'legacy' once it's put out of its misery, chances are that legacy will be the Brexit Party.

Right now, there appear to be just two parties unashamedly honest in their intentions – Farage's lot and Old Mother Cable's wet blankets. The Lib Dem's 'Stop Brexit' posts dotted around suburban grass verges – or indeed their attempt at wooing the proles, 'Bollocks to Brexit' – is a rare example of plain-speaking in a political culture wracked with doublethink rhetoric. At least the Lib Dems aren't masking their Remoaner agenda in unconvincing pretensions to a 'Brexit for all' fantasy; that's been half the problem with May, not to mention Corbyn's crowd, which is why both are being deserted by once-loyal constituencies that voted Leave in 2016. This is a mess entirely of the political class's making, and the fact so many members of it still don't understand – either by demanding a second referendum or simply pretending nobody can discern the fact they're Remainers in Leave clothing – not only shows they have learnt nothing but that they are utterly incapable of learning *anything*.

The political class and their ideological allies, the media class, can see the writing on the wall, but they don't want to read it; so, they resort to clutching at any straw they can magic-up. Indulging in daily smears against their opponents or ordering an investigation into the Brexit Party's funding that has found no evidence of wrongdoing any different from the far-from saintly way most political parties are funded – none of these tired tactics are working for anyone other than Farage. Every dairy-based beverage aimed in his direction only serves to guarantee another dozen votes for his party come tomorrow; the political and media classes are pouring petrol on the bonfire and can't figure out why their actions aren't putting out the flames.

Presiding over the longest unbroken parliament since the English Civil War, Theresa May and her rump rabble will one day give us a cracking six-part Sunday night serial, for the Watergate factor of government-in-meltdown makes for a far more engrossing drama than one about an administration winning landslides. There's never been a shortage of dramatisations of Thatcher's fall from power, for example; but who would want to watch one based around the 1987 General Election? At this moment in time, however, we aren't watching the meltdown of May from the distance of decades and wondering if they picked the right cast to play her motley crew; it's happening for real right in front of us – and the only definite outcome of *this* drama is that Theresa is toast.

BLUE TURNS TO GREY
25 May 2019

Okay, I don't doubt our favourite pocket Trotsky Owen Jones has already expressed the same sentiments; but it's pretty hard to avoid remembering there were no public tears for the 72 lives lost in the Grenfell Tower inferno, no public tears for the pensioners deported to the West Indies after half-a-century as British residents, and no public tears for the sick pushed to the brink by benefits sanctions. Instead, Theresa saved her public tears for Theresa. I don't believe public tears have a place in public life, anyway; but if you're going to cry on camera, at least do it for something other than self-pity. Perhaps the soon-to-be ex-Prime Minster belatedly realised her own limitations and the shocking realisation overwhelmed her. Somehow, though, I doubt it.

As was confirmed by a scientific study earlier in the week, those cursed with overconfidence severely overestimate their own abilities. Not only that; they are also incapable of recognising incompetence in themselves and instinctively blame their own failings on those around them. Theresa May's tunnel-vision persistence in repeatedly pushing her Brexit bill through Parliament and paying no heed to the fact that the majority of MPs kept rejecting it was an action characteristic of an individual afflicted with this syndrome, one so prevalent in her profession.

45

May's bunker mentality the day before finally putting the country (and her career) out of its misery also spoke volumes; the prospect of being confronted by colleagues telling her what she couldn't even admit to herself was something she evidently couldn't handle; and so she shut up shop until eventually emerging before the machinegun-fire of the flashbulbs yesterday to announce she was resigning. It was a bit like someone rushing up to you and excitedly telling you the final score of a football match you'd watched on TV months ago. We were all there long before she was.

Theresa May is now poised to take her place on numerous unenviable lists. She joins the likes of Neville Chamberlain, Anthony Eden, Alec Douglas-Home, Jim Callaghan and Gordon Brown as being a Prime Minister whose tenure at No.10 numbered three years or less. She also joins the likes of Ted Heath, Margaret Thatcher and Iain Duncan Smith as a Tory leader forced to fall on her sword by her own party. And, of course, she joins several names featuring on both lists as arguably the worst holder of her office in recent history. Even Prime Ministers whose most notable legacies are extremely contentious ones – Heath taking us into Europe and Cameron kick-starting the process of taking us out, to name but two – still managed to achieve something, regardless of how divisive those achievements remain. Theresa May has achieved nothing other than making a bad situation even worse than it was when she began.

There's been much talk of 'pressure' via the media post-mortems over the last 24 hours – and when one thinks of Mrs May's haggard appearance and borderline Bonnie Tyler rasp, it's undeniable the stress of the job has left its mark on her. But we shouldn't forget Theresa May didn't become Prime Minister by accident; she went for it; she wanted it. It was her choice to run for the Tory leadership, knowing she would be

PM if she won it and that the chalice passed on by her predecessor was so poisoned it was practically radioactive. Sympathy should be reserved for those who have no part to play in their misfortunes, not those who actively put themselves in a position that serves as an invitation to misfortune. One can only really pity Theresa May to any extent if one believes her delusional faith in her capabilities to do the job she grabbed with both hands is a character trait worthy of pity.

The limitations of this personality-free zone lacking the charisma and communication skills so crucial to leading both a political party and the nation were never better exposed than during the memorable car-crash of the 2017 General Election campaign. It was clear then that here was a person incurably shy, awkward and uncomfortable when under the unforgiving media spotlight; fair enough – not everybody is suited for that spotlight. But, as with a member of the public voluntarily standing before the Cowell panel, Theresa May knew the rules when she entered the game; she can't then court sympathy when she's caught out. An unimaginative box-ticking book-keeper happier maintaining mystique and avoiding public scrutiny can function fine in the Westminster shadows, but you can't switch on the lights and expect them to suddenly transform into a showman like Tony Blair. You might have been able to get away with it a century ago, but in *this* day and age?

For a vicar's daughter who once stood before her own party members and belatedly informed them that everyone outside Conservative circles viewed them as 'nasty', Theresa May's six years as Home Secretary didn't demonstrate much in the way of Christian charity. In 2013, lest we forget, she sanctioned those infamous vans bearing advertising hoardings ordering illegal immigrants to 'go home or face arrest', touring London boroughs with a high ethnic population in the same way the National Front used to target specific neighbourhoods to march through. This was scaremongering on a scale even Nigel Farage has never managed; we should remember Theresa May has played her own not-insignificant part in fostering the current hostile climate politicians are now so prone to decrying as if they were entirely blameless. Her disastrous three years as PM and her humiliating, undignified exit could be seen as a form of payback; and the supply of sympathy for her is probably as short in clubs that cater for golfers as much as clubs that cater for working-men.

One could try to be magnanimous in the face of an individual's evident anguish as her failings finally catch up with her – especially when those loathsome members of the Cabinet issuing hollow tributes to the boss whose dwindling authority they undermined at every opportunity have been openly (and shamelessly) jostling for her job for months. But the closing chapter of this sorry saga was written the same day as its author proclaimed 'Once upon a time'. Watching a Remainer like May pretending to implement something so opposed to her ideology was akin to watching a match-fixing goalkeeper trying to make the goals he throws in the back of the net look like accidents. She's got another month-and-a-bit as our alleged PM, but the reign is over; and in the event of the favourite winning the race to step into her kitten heels, we have the prospect of a tenant at No.10 from whom no one in their right mind would buy a used car. To paraphrase a far more distinguished predecessor, this ain't the beginning of the end – more like the end of the beginning.

'Unprecedented' is the ultimate hard-on word that overexcited political reporters are fond of using whenever they want to up the dramatic ante; but in this particular case it really is unavoidable. Yes, these are elections to the European Parliament and, let's be honest: many don't normally even bother to register their vote, and MEPs (bar Nigel Farage and Daniel Hannan) are usually the most anonymous politicians in the country. But it's worth remembering this has been the first occasion since the 2017 General Election that the British electorate have had clear Leave and Remain choices on the ballot paper, and the electorate have responded accordingly. The Brexit Party won in all the English regions bar London and also won Wales, even finishing runners-up to the SNP north of the border. When one takes into account the fact that the Brexit Party is *only six weeks old,* the comprehensive victory it has achieved is genuinely...well...unprecedented. 38% of the vote, 29 MEPs – remarkable.

The rapid rise of the Brexit Party and the resurgence of the Lib Dems – the only political parties (in England, at least) whose intentions are blatantly honest – can be seen as both a rejection of doublethink spin and as further evidence of electoral dissatisfaction with Labour and the Tories. The 2016 ballot paper provided the visitor to the polling booth with a straightforward in/out choice, and the public mood is still one that sees the most divisive issue of our times in simple black & white terms; despite ongoing attempts by the two main parties to wrap it in endless complexities as an example of how they're clever and we're not, voters in the European Elections have kept it simple, and who they chose to vote for reflects this. They either want to leave or they want to remain – just like they did three years ago. The fact the majority opted for the former in 2016 and yet we still haven't left means a degree in rocket science isn't necessary when wondering why a party that didn't even exist a couple of months ago has swept the Brussels board.

Political divisions in Britain for a hundred years or more have been between left and right or Labour and Conservative – ideological and party allegiances that have shaped the landscape. Yet we now appear to have returned to the factions and groupings of the 18th century, whereas instead of being a Whig or a Tory, you're now a Brexiteer or a Remainer – and whether you happen to lean to the left or dress to the right has no bearing on that. Granted, old habits find dying harder come a General Election, but the outcome of this Euro vote we shouldn't even have taken part in has demonstrated – far more than the recent local results – just how much tradition has gone for a Burton. Yes, protest votes have always been a way of venting a grievance with one's preferred party in a local or by-election; but to have so many prominent mouthpieces for both Labour and the Conservatives openly declaring they would vote against their own parties has been a notable departure from the script, especially considering how both are in such dire need of a cuddle from old friends.

It has to be said, the Lib Dems deserve credit for the way in which they have capitalised on the mixed messages coming from the big two and have essentially reinvented and rebranded themselves as the Remain Party. 'Stop Brexit' (if you live in a home-owning neighbourhood) and 'Bollocks to Brexit' (if you emanate from a council estate) have been their short, snappy slogans in a campaign they have managed with unexpectedly canny genius. They picked up on the fact that the public wanted straight-talking and, seeing how Leavers suddenly had a focus with the swift formation of Farage's colourful coalition, they gave Remainers a party of their own too.

Even the anticipated splitting of the Remain vote via the conceited deserters formerly known as TIG failed to materialise; the spectacular failure of the vanity project that is Change UK (and is it mere coincidence that their name when abbreviated reads as 'CHUK'?) has been the sole crumb of comfort for the Conservatives as this pitiful party, along with the obliterated UKIP, has at least given Tories someone to look down on from the depths of the relegation zone they now languish in. Were any of the Change UK MPs to give their constituents the chance to comment on their defection from the parties they stood for in 2017, I wonder how many would be returned to Parliament? The likelihood of any by-elections in those constituencies seems more remote than ever today.

Not that anyone was expecting unbiased reporting, but the BBC coverage of the election results not only saw amusing straw-clutching when desperately combining all non-Brexit Party votes as evidence that the country now favours Remain; there was also the persistent and irritating inference that all Brexit Party votes were gained via a simple transfusion from UKIP – as though the party was Milton Keynes Dons inheriting the history and club records of Wimbledon FC and it was all down to mere rebranding. Well, to use the language of the Lib Dems, bollocks. The Brexit Party isn't simply UKIP under another name. It may well have sucked-up the share of the vote that went to Farage's former vehicle five years ago, but by presenting itself as the only unambiguous option available to Leavers, the party has attracted thousands of disillusioned Labour and Tory voters who have simmered and seethed when watching the MPs they voted into office two years ago either dither or deliberately obstruct the implementation of something they swore they would honour.

With 11 of the UK's 12 regions declared at the time of writing, the only areas in which the Brexit Party failed to win the most votes were Scotland and London – yet, even in the Labour-centric capital, it was the Lib Dems rather than Corbyn's crew that topped the table, amusingly hitting No.1 in the Islington charts as well. It was a disastrous night for Labour – pushed into third place in Wales and falling behind the Greens in the East of England as well as the South East and the South West. The piss-poor showing by Labour will heap further pressure on beleaguered Jezza by the Watson/Starmer/Thornberry Remainer triumvirate to go all-out for a second referendum strategy, which should play out well in the party's old northern strongholds. But maybe it's already too late; Labour have spent so long sitting on that fence that the Lib Dems have steamed ahead as the party of Remain and look set to...erm...remain.

As for the Tories, well, was anyone really surprised? The Conservatives didn't win a single area and cannot finish any higher than fifth place when all the nationwide votes are tallied; the party can now boast a paltry four MEPs following a record low of 9.1% share of the vote; it's the worst result in the party's history – ever; and the Tories have a longer history than any other political party. Whoever succeeds Theresa May not only has to contend with the ever-present albeit largely imaginary threat of Corbyn; he/she also has to contend with the far more realistic threat of Nigel Farage...again – and look what that threat did to the Tories three years ago.

URBAN MYTHOLOGY
10 June 2019

Whilst the majority of last week's D-Day anniversaries were fitting tributes to those who fought them on the beaches, it was inevitable a degree of nostalgia – even for such dark days

– would creep into the commemorations. In the case of the Second World War, we have the comforting hindsight of a happy ending, which participants were denied at the time; but nostalgia – whether for the War via 'Dad's Army' or talking-heads TV celebrating more recent cultural epochs – is a romantic electric blanket that is at its warmest when the chilly present seems to lack certainties. There don't appear to be any certainties at all right now, and nobody has any idea what comes next other than predicting the worst. By contrast, the past is a benevolent piece of furniture we can curl up in and know where we are.

That said, distance sometimes enables us to discern jewels that were hidden when we were busy living in the past – as Jethro Tull once perhaps pointed out. For example, I'd only have to glance at a handful of posts on here from 2016 to come to the conclusion that 2016 was a terrible year – yet, from my own personal 2019 perspective, I can now see it was one of the happiest times of my life. If anything, this serves as a salient lesson to enjoy what one has whilst one has it instead of waiting for it to be claimed by nostalgia and the belated appreciation that is tinged with wistful regret. But I digress.

When watching the 60s/70s drama 'Public Eye' recently, it was telling that, amidst the inevitable presence of so many elements of British life long since gone, a particular plotline caught my eye: Lead character Frank Marker moves from one town to another and has to make an appointment to meet the man who is now his bank manager in order that his account can be transferred from his old branch to his new one. Despite Reg Varney making history with his inaugural withdrawal in 1967, hole-in-the-wall cash machines were hardly a fixture on every street corner through the 1970s, if at all. Alfred Burke's character couldn't simply relocate elsewhere and continue to withdraw money from anywhere he happened to be – neither could he manage his financial affairs himself online; all of his payments were physical and if he wanted to invest or withdraw, he needed to go to an actual building and make the exchange over the counter by engaging with a fellow human being.

In a week in which I witnessed the doors of yet another neighbourhood bank branch close for good, this scene from 'Public Eye' also reminded me how that mainstay of 70s sitcom jokes, the bank manager, was once an office almost on a par with the local vicar, GP or police constable in terms of 'civic dignitaries'; they no doubt still count for something in Ambridge, but in urban areas the bank manager is virtually an extinct species. If you, like me, reside in an urban area, you won't have a bank manager either – nor do you probably know a vicar, a copper or even a GP, at least if your experience of the impersonal surgeries in which a different doctor dispenses medication every time you visit is anything like mine.

In most cases, the clout such professions carried has gone because the environment that elevated them has gone. The absence of belonging that many in an alienating metropolis feel can partly be traced back to the point where the strands of benign authority that helped bind communities together became frayed and then snapped; from village elder to local squire to Sgt Dixon, the people required at least one go-to figure to resolve their disputes. Even if they still do, those figures aren't around anymore; and, anyway, if authority equates with age, the village elder is most likely now rotting away in a care home. We can't rely on the police to come running when we dial 999, we can't get an appointment to see a GP, and our bank no longer has a branch on the high-street. Even if you favour collectivism, you'd be hard pushed to generate it in such a fragmented landscape.

The old concept of community, in which everyone had a part to play and a function to perform, had developed from the village roots of towns and had in turn arisen from ancient tribal divisions of labour; in those parts of the world where the literal meaning of 'tribe' still applies, one tends to find these roles remain intact and crucial to the community's survival. In the west, where communities had grown through being supported and sustained by one specific industry, a sense of place was strong in a way that – following the subsequent black hole of underinvestment since the industry's collapse – has been rendered utterly redundant. A town's residents can connect with someone on the other side of the world but might not necessarily know a single person living on their street.

Today, community can be more of abstract concept, often equating with identity; the general trend is for the rejection of shared common ground in favour of individual separateness. Even when people defined by their differences or 'diversity' are quick to gather in a facsimile of community, their emphasis on individuality precludes genuine community, hence the endless splitting into endless subdivisions of every community based around identity, underlining how diversity can diversify to the point whereby nobody has anything in common anymore. The 21st century incarnations of the People's Front of Judea and the Judean People's Front are permanently engaged in social media spats that make unity seem like something people only did in the old days. We receive a tantalising taste of it when we pause to commemorate lives lost in conflicts that required unity to succeed; but the fact that WWII will soon cease inhabiting living memory to join the Napoleonic Wars as mere history keeps it firmly in the context of the past.

Politicians being, of course, the cynical old manipulators of the public mood that they instinctively are, sell themselves to the electorate by appealing to the craving for community as it used to be. The pitches of the wretched hopefuls vying to become the new Tory leader (and, unfortunately, Prime Minister) are crammed with fatuous references to 'bringing the nation together' as they line-up like a bunch of vacuous suits to be sneered at by Alan Sugar. The fact that they all appear to be falling over each other to see who can produce the best drug-taking anecdote is a bizarre development that could be viewed as either an attempt to appear human (not easy for a Conservative MP) or to pre-empt any dirty digging on the part of their opponents. Personally, my opinion of Michael Gove has not changed one iota now that I know he snorted coke 20 years ago; and to be honest, if I was married to Sarah Vine I'd probably be permanently off my tits on mushrooms, seeing that as the only viable means of achieving domestic bliss.

Understandably, one response to this strange rash of substance abuse confessions from the kind of people you really don't want to picture snorting or skinning-up has been accusations of hypocrisy. For decades, the Conservative Party has repeatedly opposed any grownup discussions on the antiquated drugs laws and has constantly played the finger-wagging nanny against anyone daring to recreationally indulge. Then again, this 'do as I say, not as I do' approach that the current confessions appear to emphasise is perhaps especially grating because it sounds so parental, albeit emanating from the most uncaring and irresponsible parents imaginable. If we need our village elders today, Westminster is not the village where we'll find them.

I wonder if, when the ex-Iron Chancellor eventually ascends to that great No.11 in the sky, his headstone will read: 'Gordon Brown – he agreed with Nick'? Ever since the inaugural 2010 Leaders' Debate, it's become obligatory for contenders in a party political contest to set out their respective stalls against each other for the electorate via the goggle-box, and there's usually a specific moment that catches the electorate's ear during a debate – even if, in the case of the Tory leadership pitches televised by BBC1 and Channel 4, most of us have no say in what happens next; these guys really are preaching exclusively to the converted. Yes, there was a Labour precedent three years ago when Owen Smith was pitted against Jeremy Corbyn in a 'Question Time' special as the former staged a hapless challenge to the latter's leadership; but the number of participants in the Tories' current competition has inevitably upped the 'Apprentice' ante, speaking a visual language familiar to the viewing public.

The first debate on Sunday served as a belated reminder of just how threadbare the Tory talent pool really is – and the contentious individual whose coronation seems a foregone conclusion didn't even make an appearance. As entertainment, it was a bit like watching the political equivalent of one of those NME Poll Winners' concerts from the mid-60s, albeit one in which The Beatles, Stones and Kinks had all pulled-out at the last minute, leaving the punters to make do with Freddie and the Dreamers, The Honeycombs and The Four Pennies (ask Paul Gambaccini). Deliberately leaving an empty lectern to emphasise the favourite's no-show could have been even funnier had the director opted for a 'HIGNFY' Hattersley moment and placed a tub of lard on top of it; but the viewers probably wouldn't have noticed the difference, anyway.

Of the inferior five who were helplessly hoping to chip away at Boris's unassailable lead last Sunday, Dominic Raab reminds me of a wooden hunk from a daytime TV soap – the sort-of wife-cheating character who says things like 'Ruth, I didn't set out to hurt you'; whereas Jeremy Hunt resembles a smooth regional news magazine presenter, the kind the grannies always think is 'lovely'. The strangely simian Rory Stewart looks like he'd be at his happiest playing in war games tournaments with his model soldiers, whilst I keep imagining Sajid Javid as a member of staff stationed on the aisles in Wilkos, the slightly gormless one a little over-eager to help when you can't find where the loo rolls have been moved to. And then there's the new pseudo-macho Michael Gove, who nevertheless never looks like anyone other than Michael Gove. God didn't make two.

Jeremy Hunt's 'Where's Boris?' question halfway through the first debate was the first time any of the five mentioned the missing member, and the question almost sounded like a euphemism for an ill-timed fart, as though Hunt had accidentally released a Tommy Squeaker and used a Tory codeword to own-up; anyone whose father used to ask 'Who's let Polly out of prison?' whenever a silent-but-deadly odour infected a car journey will get what I mean. Actually, maybe if the whole nation got into the habit of shouting 'Where's Boris?' whenever a fart slipped out in company, the nation might become more of a One Nation in the process. But I think we've already passed that point now; we probably passed it when Harold Macmillan resigned in 1963.

The fact that such a tiny proportion of the electorate actually gets to vote in this particular contest leaves it a curiously meaningless spectacle for the rest of us – and on both the lectern incarnation and the Beeb's 'casual bar-stools' version, it seemed as if the contestants were equally confused by their target audience. They each performed as they would during a General Election campaign, as though canvassing the entire nation for votes rather than the select few who'll receive a ballot paper; moreover, the contenders often appeared to forget that in bemoaning the state of the nation they were actually trashing their own party's record in government, not the opposition (despite Gove's lone 'Jezza-phobic' howl). All emphasised the pitiful state of public services that many of them have been responsible for the pitiful state of, and all promised to wave a magic wand that all have kept well-hidden whilst endorsing the wrecking-ball that has helped make this country what it is over the past decade. Lest we forget, whoever gets the gig will inherit the same shambles that stitched-up their predecessor, so it's not as if they can deliver any promises without a mandate of their own – and they'll resist getting one for as long as they can because they're terrified of calling a General Election they're convinced they'll lose.

The second debate dispensed with the first's studio audience and instead had questions put by members of the public via a video screen; unfortunately, there was no moment comparable to that when a housewife riled Margaret Thatcher with an awkward inquiry about the Belgrano back on 'Nationwide' in 1983, though with one of the questions being put by a bearded chap representing a certain community, it was inevitable Emily Maitlis turned to Boris. Yes, with Raab the plank having been eliminated just a couple of hours before the BBC1 debate, his replacement was the man whose dominance in the first two ballots necessitated his appearance; I almost expected him to wait until the rest were assembled before descending to the stage on the zip-wire he famously hung from when promoting the 2012 London Olympics, but he didn't, alas. The manner in which Boris's propensity for putting his foot in it has been reduced by the simple tactic of turning him into Howard Hughes is certainly a bizarre approach for a man who will have nowhere to hide once he enters No.10. But Claudius finally has his chance to show a clown can become Caesar, and the luxury of mediocre competition means he can do so however he wants.

Viewing the BBC2 series on Margaret Thatcher these past few weeks has served as a reminder how politics used to be run by serious grownups; regardless of the still-divisive ideology at the heart of the Thatcher revolution – many elements of which remain open to question – there was at least a vision inherent in the rhetoric, even if its worst aspects are responsible for those vying for the top job in 2019. Had today's template applied in the 1970s, the Tories would have been led by Sir Gerald Nabarro; Nabarro was the reactionary, racist buffoon with the handlebar moustache who had become a household name on account of the larger-than-life, comic toff he presented to the public. It's fair to say he lacked certain qualities that were then regarded as essential to become a party leader. However, perhaps telling of the times, Nabarro's character – midway between Jimmy Edwards and Colonel Blimp – was a complete fabrication, for he was actually the state-educated son of a shopkeeper. And *that's* what would disqualify him today.

Acting out its existential crisis in public by presenting pitches to a public that cannot respond to them, the Conservative Party seems to be contradicting the stated aims of the leadership hopefuls to 'bring the nation together' by allowing us all to see how dysfunctional the party proposing to do so really is. In publicly attempting to outshine not opponents from other political parties, but fellow Tory MPs and (in most cases) Cabinet colleagues, the contenders underlined just how David Cameron's suspension of collective responsibility in 2016 has now become the norm. But at least the Tories are an accurate barometer of the disunited kingdom as it currently stands rather than a source of optimism for an imaginary united future.

CREAM OF THE CRAP
25 June 2019

I can't quite decide if this reboot of 'Yes, Prime Minister' is funnier than the original or if I'm laughing in all the wrong places, what with it having adopted the pseudo-documentary style of 'The Thick of It', a tactic which can throw the viewer. This week's was a classic episode, however; in case you missed it, that rather implausible comic character called Boris had a blazing row with his girlfriend – though unbeknownst to him it was being recorded by a Remainer neighbour, who then flogged it to the Guardian! All kinds of hilarity ensued, with Boris, under pressure from his weedy workplace colleague Jeremy (the) Cunt, refusing to answer questions on the matter via the rib-tickling route of talking over whoever asked the question. Well worth a watch if you can locate it on the iPlayer.

I would say 'but seriously' if that didn't seem out of kilter with the comedy narrative – but *seriously,* this would be a highly entertaining shit-show if there wasn't so much at stake. With Michael Gove suspiciously edged out of the race, the sole obstacle between Boris Johnson and No.10 would appear to be Boris Johnson – and whilst Boris's team are doing their best to present him as a responsible politician with a vision as they prepare for his coronation, there's only so much they can control once the man himself is under the spotlight they've tried to keep him out of. At the same time, there are some unsurprisingly dirty tricks at play on both sides right now; the tactical voting that eliminated the man who destroyed Boris's bid three years ago belatedly brought a touch of Westminster Dark Arts to proceedings.

Smarmy little troll he may well be, but Gove was the one contender who could have really gone for the jugular – and Boris's team knew it. However, the convenient timing of last weekend's developments has shown the Hunt camp is taking a sneakier approach. Knowing all-too well that Bo-Jo's chaotic private life is as prone to gaffes as his public life, his enemies have probably been on stand-by ever since the race gathered pace, anticipating an incident that can then be weaponised as further evidence of Boris's unsuitability for high office. They didn't have long to wait. They received it thanks to the unique Neighbourhood Watch scheme in operation on Carrie Symonds' street; and the added bonus of a 'domestic abuse' angle also gave the green light to opportunistic Opposition gobshites like Jess Phillips to accelerate the anti-Boris campaign.

However, simplifying the contest to a one-sided battle between the school swot and the school bully tends to obscure the ammunition that could be used by the favourite against the outsider. As a relatively loyal member of Mrs May's far-from devoted Cabinet, Jeremy Hunt offers a similar 'safe pair of hands' option that the outgoing PM presented in 2016. But it says a lot about where we are now that Hunt's shameful role in News Corporation's attempted takeover of BSkyB back in 2011 – not to mention his far-from illustrious record as Health Secretary – has been barely mentioned by his opponent's team, so confident of success that they haven't even thought it necessary to hurl a few stones from their glass house. The irony is that Hunt has more than enough skeletons in his closet to keep them busy, and they may have to resort to them if the headlines continue to bring Boris's numerous failings into focus.

Tony Benn's wife Caroline once said that Prime Ministers generally fall into one of three categories: Pedestrians, Fixers or Madmen. What we know of both the former Foreign Secretary and the incumbent one suggests neither fits the middle description, so the choice would appear to be Pedestrian or Madman. A strong Opposition would have rendered the Tories' squabbles irrelevant, mind; they'd be so far behind in the polls that a successful vote of no confidence in a no-deal Brexit Boris would trigger a General Election and throw the party out of office – giving Boris the shortest premiership in history, breaking the unenviable 119 days of George Canning in 1827 (though the duelling PM did have the excuse of his tenure being curtailed by death). But, of course, this isn't a Labour Party led by Harold Wilson that can boast heavyweights of the calibre of Jenkins, Callaghan, Castle, Crosland, Healey, Benn and Foot; it's Jezza's frontbench of Watson, Starmer, Abbott and Thornberry. This is the team the Tories are so terrified of that they will back Boris at all costs. This is what it has come to.

Under normal circumstances, Bo-Jo presents any opponent with such an embarrassment of riches to use against him that the mere thought of him running for PM would be a non-starter from the off; under normal circumstances, he would never have got this far. But these are not normal circumstances. Lest we forget, three years ago a majority of the electorate voted to leave the EU; three years later, we still haven't left. The ramifications of Brexit have now claimed two Prime Ministers and judging by Boris's performance on the hustings, a third scalp is on the cards. After one disastrous dullard, the Conservative fear of a Corbyn Government will most likely avoid another and instead opt for a rogue – even if there's more to it than a straightforward scrap with Mr Nice Guy on one side and Mr 'I wouldn't trust him with my wallet or my wife' on the other.

Then again, it's not as if we haven't had rogues at No.10 before; the gallery of past Prime Ministers lining the wall beside the Downing Street staircase contains its fair share of reprobates even Boris Johnson would struggle to compete with. The Duke of Grafton (PM 1768-70) paraded his courtesan mistress around society whilst his wife the Duchess had a baby with her paramour; Lord Melbourne (PM 1834-41) had been married to Byron's insane lover Lady Caroline Lamb and had himself been blackmailed in a sex scandal; and Lord Palmerston (PM 1855-65) was known to have fathered his own 'love children' as well as being cited in divorce proceedings. So, it's fair to say we have been here before. But, certainly in the case of Palmerston, there was substantial substance beneath the superficial surface; can that honestly be said of a self-serving, ideological vacuum like Boris, whose track record in office is laughable?

By disregarding its traditional support systems and courting the favour of minority metropolitan causes, the political class on both sides has created the monster that is Boris, just as American Democrats created Trump. Whether Tories abandoning the small-c conservative shires or Labour doing likewise with the deindustrialised working-classes, this abandonment has had its ultimate expression in Brexit; the fact that, three bloody years on, we still haven't moved proves the political class has learnt nothing. The impasse that is entirely of the political class's making has given the kiss of life to Nigel Farage and is poised to make Boris f***ing Johnson Prime Minister. You reap what you sow, Westminster. It's just a shame the rest of us will again have to pay for your wretched incompetence.

It's a toss-up as to which is the most undignified gesture, really – gate-crashing Europe's leading gentleman's club with a choreographed stunt during the playing of 'Ode to Joy', or wearing T-shirts bearing the legend 'Bollocks to Brexit'. It'd be comforting to think the former was a protest at Ludwig Van's masterpiece being purloined for political purposes, but alas, no, for these are our representatives on the European stage in 2019; it's enough to make one hanker for Brotherhood of Man and Buck's Fizz. Then again, representatives for both sides of the divide advertised their intentions in advance, or at least the respective stances they would take once in a) The Lion's Den or b) The Garden of Eden (tick where applicable).

The Brexit Party certainly made it clear they planned to descend upon the European Parliament determined to disrupt proceedings in the manner of Paisleyite Unionists striding into 1970s Westminster; similarly, the servile sucking-up to the same institution by their Lib Dem opponents whilst wearing their contempt for democracy as a literal T-shirt (just in case anybody missed it) shouldn't have come as a surprise either. Of course, three years ago 17 million members of the Great British electorate decided we wouldn't be sending any MEPs to Brussels in 2019; but the fact we are means it was almost inevitable the conflicting responses of the British intake would be akin to children being let loose in an adventure playground without parental supervision. That's where we are now.

Whether 'Carry On Up The EU', milkshakes as missiles, baby blimps hovering over London, or every Grauniad reader's favourite 'Urban' person Stormzy leading a white woke audience in a chant of 'Fuck Boris' at the rock & pop Glyndebourne known as Glastonbury, it would appear the nation is experiencing its second childhood. The default panic room when faced with the intractable series of crises confronting the country seems to be the nursery. People are worried about the future, impoverished by Austerity, browbeaten by Brexit and powerless in the face of Parliament discarding its democratic duty, so they retreat to the sole surviving safe-space available to them – sticking their tongues out at the powers-that-be en route, and shouting 'Fascist', 'Nazi' or 'Racist' for good measure.

Reduced to hurling an aforementioned dairy-based beverage at a pantomime villain when the ability to articulate frustration any other way appears a lost art – that's 2019; the argument has exhausted the nation, even though most of us ironically do now know a great deal more about the EU than when presented with a choice in 2016. Unfortunately, those of a Second Referendum bent have failed to realise that possession of this knowledge doesn't necessarily serve as the ideal recruitment weapon for the Remainer narrative; if anything, the more we learn the more likely we are to be drawn to the Leave cause. They really should've retained the beguiling mystique of the EU and not exposed the grotesque bureaucratic behemoth to the light.

At least we all had a say in 2016 (even if it appears to have counted for nothing in the end) – unlike the race to No.10, the latest offshoot from Cameron's can of worms. Yet, if eras are given leaders most pertinent to those eras, perhaps it shouldn't come as a great surprise that Boris Johnson is still the odds-on favourite to be the next Prime Minister. He is the ideal candidate for our times – immature, immoral, avaricious, frivolous, reckless, devious, dishonest – and so say all of us. Maybe the most significant example to date of Boris's inability to cope in a crisis came via his infamously sloppy response to the detainment and imprisonment of Nazanin Zaghari-Ratcliffe; the potential damage the then-Foreign Secretary's casual comments did to the British-Iranian citizen held on dubious spying charges in Tehran contrast sharply with Jim Callaghan's response to the threatened execution of Ugandan-based British author and lecturer Denis Hills in 1975. Hills was sentenced to death by firing squad on charges of espionage and sedition; but Callaghan as Foreign Secretary made a personal approach to Idi Amin, flying out to Kampala and bringing Hills home. That's the kind of thing grownups do – or *used* to.

An elderly, ailing Churchill returning to power in 1951 was the perfect personification of the early 50s malaise, playing the nation's grandfather in the manner of an aged stationmaster from the Rev. W. Awdry's Railway Series; Harold Wilson was the right man for the job in 1964, surfing the wave of the nation's dynamic go-getting attitude via his utilisation of both the pre-eminent pop culture and the white heat of the new technology; he performed his own late Churchill role ten years later, holding both party and country together as one last duty before collecting his carriage clock; in contrast, the big hair & big shoulder pad ensemble of Mrs Thatcher was the stylistic embodiment of mid-80s excess in all its 'greed-is-good' vulgarity as the free-market hounds were released for round one of casino capitalism's ascendancy; the middle-management, superficial blandness of Blair and his heir, Cameron, equally made them men of their times. We've got Boris.

Yes, like Trump, he may piss-off the right-on chattering classes – which is undeniably entertaining; but that's not a good enough reason on its own to hand him the keys to No.10. We should be able to do better. But take a look at the opposing frontbenches and nominate a great man or woman who would make a great leader. No, me neither. This is an age of unprecedented parliamentary mediocrities. Boris has always caught the eye because of the amusing comic character he plays in public; surrounded by such nonentities, he was bound to stand out. But the Enoch Powell-like 'voice in the wilderness' aura he has generated from the backbenches ever since his exit from government should have kept him as a perennial beacon for mischief-makers to congregate around, not propel him all the way to Downing Street.

Boris wants to be Prime Minister, whereas Nigel Farage claims he doesn't want to be an MEP; his presence in Brussels inevitably provokes cries of hypocrisy from his enemies. 'But you still collect your Brussels salary!' Yes, just like all those SNP MPs whose avowed aim is to detach their country from the UK and its parliament, yet still receive their Westminster paycheque – or all the members of the Northern Ireland Executive who continue to be paid, despite the fact it hasn't sat at Stormont for over two years. Nice work if you can get it, eh? All adult avenues are sealed-off now, so while you arm yourself with a milkshake, I shall continue to exercise my own puerile prodding with the occasional silly, satirical video as I proceed towards my destiny as Miss Havisham. Or maybe not...

OH, WHAT A LOVELY WAR!
9 July 2019

For the Tories, one could opt for 1945, 1966 or 1974 – and especially that 13-year period from 1997-2010 when a succession of pitiful team captains were dispatched to the crease to chase an impossible target. For Labour, the options are myriad: 1959, 1970, 1979, 1983 etc....all the way up to 2015. Yes, the two political parties that have dictated the destiny of the nation over the last century have each known their fallow periods; the scales have risen and fallen in favour of one or the other throughout the past 100 years, sometimes the victor dependent on alliances with third parties, sometimes going it alone with the cushion of a landslide – though one could argue only Clement Attlee and Margaret Thatcher really took advantage of the numbers and went for it.

What makes the here and now so strangely incompatible with the manual is that the traditional narrative of one party soaring in strength whilst the other struggles in shambolic disarray isn't happening. Instead, the twin titans that have bestrode the British political landscape for longer than any of us has been alive are crammed into the one canoe, zooming up shit creek, having misplaced the proverbial paddle. It's quite a spectacle. We're used to the usual internal evisceration that occurs in the wake of a party crashing at the ballot-box; it generally takes half-a-decade before the right man or woman emerges to put the house in order and make the losers electable again; by the time this happens, the cracks that the party in office papered-over with victory are beginning to be exposed to the light, and defeat awaits before the game of pass-the-parcel resumes. *That's* what we're used to.

To see both the Conservative Party and the Labour Party going through their crises in-synch is bizarre because it's so unprecedented. The Tories' travails stretch back further than Brexit – Cameron's Blaire-lite approach to social issues (usually involving the word 'gay') didn't play well with the retired admirals and blue-rinsed battleaxes out in the Shires - but any grumblings were subdued by the sight of 'Red' Ed sitting on the opposition benches. The spectre of Europe, however – the bad smell that just won't leave the golf-club – was bound to resurface as an open fire for dissidents to cluster around, and Dave appeased them with a bright idea largely devised to stem the flow in the direction of UKIP. It not only cost Cameron his job; it may well yet obliterate his party.

As for Labour, the lurch to the left that came with Corbyn and his Marxist groupies was accompanied by a successful recruitment drive that his acolytes were fond of quoting whenever Jezza's unpopularity beyond the student debating society was mentioned. The problem with marketing Jeremy Corbyn as a fashion accessory was that fashion has a habit of dating quickly, and it seems Jezza-mania is already 'so last year' – or, to be more accurate, the year before. It probably peaked with the defeat that was almost sold as a victory in the 2017 General Election; the party performed far better than the polls suggested, but not good enough.

For a career backbencher like Corbyn, opposition is his comfort zone; it was even when Labour were in power, as his voting record testifies; and he has constantly struggled to balance the entrenched backbench mindset with the necessary compromise of leadership. When the impetus appeared to be with Remain during the 2016 Referendum campaign, Jezza's invisibility underlined his difficulty in marrying his strong anti-Brussels stance to the pro-EU sentiments of his disciples. Stick with the latter and No.10 could beckon; but doing so would be a betrayal of the principles studied at the feet of that late, great guru and Leave sage Tony Benn.

This perennial conflict has arisen once again as the Brexit saga has grown more polarising over the past twelve months, and the humiliating ineptitude of Labour to capitalise on the Tories' civil war by failing to shoot ahead in the polls again suggests we've passed peak Jezza-mania. The rapacious appetite for power so shamelessly embodied in the loathsome person of Tom Watson has focused on the Remain cause as a means of taking back control – but from whom? The Lib

Dems? That's who Labour's U-turn on backing a second referendum has been really prompted by, not the Government.

Anti-Semitism seems to be to Labour what Europe is to the Tories, albeit something that's arguably even more difficult to deal with considering the inability of so many in the party to distinguish between the Jewish people and the Jewish State. In this respect, Europe for Labour could be viewed as a convenient smokescreen that also enables the likes of Watson, Starmer and Thornberry to exploit the issue as the best way to reconnect with the electorate when the messiah appears incapable of progressing beyond his core fan-base. The main drawback to this master-plan – endorsed by the unions (did their potentate McCluskey even sanction a ballot?) – is that it makes the same mistake as that opportunistic, clueless chameleon Umunna in assuming just because Londoners with the loudest voices wave the EU flag, they somehow represent the entire electorate.

How, one wonders, can Labour ever reconcile their metropolitan mindset with those loyal provincial supporters whose patience has been so severely tested over the last three years by allowing Bunter to hog the headlines and lead the party towards oblivion even quicker than the man whose job he's clearly after? The delusional belief of Labour's centrists that there is a vast pool of floating voters just waiting for the chance to flock around their wing of the party was embarrassingly exposed as a fallacy when that egotistical coalition of Labour and Tory defectors (what were they called again?) were utterly crushed in the European Elections. At a moment when Labour needs all the friends it can get as the Tories are imploding before our very eyes, the party is losing those whose loyalty saw Labour through many a lean decade. The Government must be watching events on the other side of the House barely able to believe their good fortune.

Of course, Brexit is a symptom of so much more, so much remaining unaddressed and unattended to by either party as each exhibits its own self-absorbed conceit at the expense of a people who have had enough. June 23 2016 was a storm long time coming, but neither party prepared by bringing a brolly. And they're still stocking-up on sunscreen rather than purchasing parkas.

THE BEECH BOY
22 July 2019

Veteran devotees of my *oeuvre* may recall a spoof documentary series that once garnered me handsome viewing figures on YouTube; titled 'Exposure', it was the beneficiary of a people's platform now gone, appearing long before Google flexed its monopolising muscles and clamped down on dissent and mischief simply because it can. Satirising the Savile-inspired paedo panic of Operation Yewtree and its very own Matthew Hopkins – i.e. failed police gargoyle Mark Williams-Thomas – the series eventually struggled to encompass the ever-expanding roll-call of opportunistic 'victims' coming forward with suspect sob stories. So many compensation claims and imaginative misery memoirs were weighing down the bandwagon by the final episode of 'Exposure' that some characters' sizeable contribution to the hysteria didn't grab centre stage until after it was all over.

'Nick' gains one or two mentions in the later 'Exposure' instalments, but he emerged too late to receive the full treatment, despite being the prime mover behind the Dolphin Square and Elm Guest House fables. He was the shady figure whose litany of personal suffering at the grubby hands of establishment abusers knew no bounds – at least according to the testimony documented with slavering relish by Exaro, a deservedly-discredited online outlet with an appetite for lurid

72

sensationalistic scandal that made the News of the World resemble the Financial Times. A few in the know were aware 'Nick' was called Carl Beech, but Beech exploited his legal anonymity to the full, safe in the knowledge that the targets of his retrospective allegations wouldn't be afforded the same courtesy.

Those who had supposedly played pivotal parts in Beech's lengthy catalogue of abuse included the obligatory Sir Jim, the former Prime Minister Edward Heath, Normandy veteran Lord Bramall, ageing ex-MPs Harvey Proctor, Leon Brittan and Lord Janner, and the former heads of MI5 and MI6 respectively, Sir Michael Hanley and Sir Maurice Oldfield. Indeed, it was remarkable how many household names and prominent figures entered Beech's childhood orbit; he was apparently never abused by nonentities. But I suppose the scenario is similar to that of the medium whose séances always seem to feature guest appearances from significant historical personalities rather than nondescript agricultural labourers. Beech's presence at incidents of abuse, torture and murder undertaken by notable public servants was apparently down to his late stepfather, an army major who passed Beech around like the proverbial parcel amongst celebrity sex-offenders at clandestine military bases. Sounds very plausible, doesn't it.

Most of us who were made aware of Beech's allegations at the time found them pretty fantastical, to say the least; some even said so and were shot down as 'paedo apologists' — though to their tenacious credit, the majority of them tirelessly carried on saying out loud what many were thinking. That their sterling efforts could be so viciously dismissed for fear they might disrupt the narrative speaks volumes, however; such was the climate. After all, Titus Oates could only have provoked the panic he managed during the reign of Charles II because anti-Catholic paranoia was so rampant; and Carl Beech was fortunate to find himself in a culture that enabled his fantasies to expand into evermore audacious areas because it wasn't just the usual conspiracy theory Icke cultists backing him up; people in positions of power were inexplicably prepared to believe too.

'Believe' was the buzzword that fuelled the false allegation industry, endorsed by the police and given the seal of approval by politicians. Keir Starmer in his DPP guise and Tom Watson in his backbench moral crusader mode are as responsible for the climate that facilitated Beech's flights of fancy as anyone and both should be hung out to dry before either gets anywhere near the leadership of the Labour Party. Watson is at it again right now, this time honing in on anti-Semites in a further bid to bolster his eventual and inevitable bid for Jezza's office; yet, even if there is an undeniable problem in Labour ranks re this issue, one can never entirely trust Bunter's motives because of the appalling role he played in the Beech-inspired 'Popish Plot' concerning a nonexistent Westminster VIP Paedophile Ring. And it was down to Watson's tedious persistence that the Metropolitan Police Force then stumbled onto the stage with fishing rods at the ready.

Operation Midland, the Met Inquisition that saw a posse of blundering Bobbies gate-crash the homes of the aged and the ailing in the full glare of the Scotland Yard PR spotlight not only besmirched and blemished the reputations of several public figures; it also caused undue distress to the families and loved ones of those they saw pass away with a stain on their names that was neither warranted nor vindicated. The rightly-notorious 'credible and true' response by the police to Carl Beech's tall tales was a characteristic reaction by those of low IQs who were entrusted to enact the letter of the law as laid out by the far smarter and utterly despicable Starmer, whose hands are probably wrapped in tight black gloves to obscure the blood on them; his Met storm-troopers vos only obeying orders, of course. For two years. At a cost of £2 million to the taxpayer. Without a single arrest.

Perhaps unsurprisingly for someone so evidently obsessed with paedos in a manner reminiscent of anti-communist witch-finders in McCarthyite America (who couldn't look under their beds without finding a Red), Carl Beech is himself a paedophile; he was found guilty earlier this year of possessing hundreds of indecent images. Fancy that. And this is someone who at one time used to visit schools on behalf of the NSPCC to lecture kiddies on how to recognise a fiddler; maybe he just walked into the classroom, pointed to himself, and then walked out. Well, he won't be an ill-advised ambassador for the charity again. As of today, Beech is a convicted fraudster as well as a paedophile, having been found guilty of 12 counts of perverting the course of justice and one count of fraud following a 10-week trial at Newcastle Crown Court. Northumbria may have made the loathsome Vera Baird its Crime Commissioner, but its police force has at least redeemed the county's reputation with this thorough investigation into a man who had outfoxed and fooled its cousins in the capital.

The law finally caught up with Carl Beech when he was arrested on the run in Sweden last year, and the verdict in Newcastle was a long time coming; but the damage done by the former NHS manager and school governor will take far longer to repair than it'll take him to serve the sentence he'll receive for his crimes. And, lest we forget, this repulsive character is merely the tip of an almighty iceberg, the vast body of which remains submerged with a thousand tragic tales to tell – tales of fathers, brothers, sons, husbands, wives, daughters, sisters and mothers, the *real* victims of this insidious cancer on contemporary society.

MASS DEBATE
24 July 2019

I've still never set foot in a betting-shop. Even though I know the old image of the grubby dive inhabited by seedy, dirty old men smoking dog-ends has received a facelift in recent years, I remain resistant to the premises' questionable charms. The only time I ever considered it was during the Blur Vs Oasis chart battle of 1995. For those too young or too indifferent, this was the moment when the nation's two rival Britpop bands rearranged their release schedules for an ingenious PR exercise that saw their new singles simultaneously hit the record-racks. I would have put money on Blur reaching the top spot because I figured your average pop fan would buy 'Country House' as well as hardcore Blur fans, whereas I correctly guessed only Oasis devotees would invest in 'Roll With It'. What this odd example is supposed to represent is the fact that you can't get to No.1 on the strength of your fan-base alone; you need the support of the masses too.

It's something Hillary Clinton failed to appreciate during the 2016 US Presidential Election campaign; dismissing a vast section of blue-collar, working-class voters as essentially illiterate idiots and then expecting to be elected without their votes was a measure of her delusional arrogance. She drove them into the arms of Trump and then couldn't understand why she didn't win. It's fine to be seen signalling your virtue by standing next to Beyoncé on a podium, but you can't get elected unless you cultivate an appeal that cuts across all the divides that Mrs Clinton's attitude exacerbated. Even if you think great swathes of the electorate are morons, you don't say it out loud; you pretend to be their friend. Once you're in office, f**k 'em; but not before. Trump laid a trap for Hillary and she walked right into it; I can't help but feel he's playing the same game at the moment as well.

His typical Twitter baiting of the so-called 'squad' of four Democrat Congresswomen last week resulted in the unedifying spectacle of a crowd chanting 'Send her back', displaying openly racist rhetoric in a political context like we haven't seen in the States (outside of a KKK rally, anyway) for half-a-century. The worldwide condemnation of the shit Trump stirred even caused the President to backtrack a little; but not much. As has been pointed out by various commentators, in choosing to take on a quartet of Democrats not necessarily representative of Democrats as a whole (one of the four has apparently expressed distinctly anti-Semitic sentiments in the past), he is cunningly re-branding the Democratic Party as a kind of Identity Politics pressure group, something that will alienate floating voters come 2020 and could well contribute towards a second term for the Donald.

Trump's new counterpart on this side of the Atlantic didn't require the electorate to be promoted to the top job, but he'll need to court their favour before long. Boris Johnson's inaugural lectern speech will probably be delivered in a way we can predict in advance, crammed with the standard vapid platitudes – just as Mrs May's was three short years ago. He will no doubt declare his intention to 'unite the nation', for the tiny majority he inherits from his predecessor will necessitate a General Election sooner rather than later and he will still have an appetite for electioneering after the interminably prolonged Tory leadership contest. He may also imagine relocating to Downing Street wipes his previous pitiful ministerial slate clean; after all, the main focus during the leadership campaign was on his stint as London Mayor –

though claiming Boris delivered the 2012 Olympics is a bit like saying Harold Wilson delivered the 1966 World Cup.

The outcome of the Tory leadership contest was the most foregone of foregone conclusions, akin to being bloated by a hearty meal and knowing the following day will inevitably open with a lengthy stint on the throne. We all knew Boris Johnson would become Prime Minister, and now he is. Just think of what that says about where we are. Anyway, the understandable outrage over the fact that the new tenant of No.10 was elected by a miniscule section of the electorate isn't that big a deal if your political memory predates Brexit. Boris got the gig like Theresa May did in 2016; and Gordon Brown in 2007; and John Major in 1990; Jim Callaghan in 1976; Sir Alec Douglas-Home in 1963...and so on. It's hardly unprecedented. The only unique aspect to this contentious succession was how desperately Mrs May dragged it out, stretching her lame duck status simply because she wanted to be PM for a few days more than Gordon Brown managed.

Other than Brexit, Boris's in-tray is interesting. The rather shameful state of the nation's maritime traditions has been highlighted by a certain incident involving Iran's piratical Revolutionary Guard; memories of how similarly swingeing cuts intended for Jolly Jack Tar's fleet were only prevented by the actions of some Argentine opportunists planting their flag on Falklands soil back in 1982 probably don't help in that this time round the cuts have already happened. And now we're paying the price. As Boris doesn't appear to believe in bugger-all but Boris, it will be fascinating to see how he responds to external events that are part-and-parcel of what a PM has to deal with. He has enough *in*ternal events on his hands with the odd 'look at me' resignation on the eve of his coronation, suggesting we should expect a Cabinet of yes-men and women. However, perhaps it's no surprise when one thinks of the collective irresponsibility of the unruly rabble his predecessor was surrounded by.

Somewhat under the radar, there's been further changing of the guard with the election of Jo Swinson as leader of the Liberal Democrats. A casualty of the electoral cull of Coalition Lib Dems in 2015, Swinson bounced back in 2017 in the same way the man she replaces did. The most striking contrast between the Party's first female leader and the guy she's succeeded comes with their respective birth certificates, however: Old Mother Cable is 76, whereas his successor is 39. Swinson seizes power at an opportune moment for the Lib Dems, fresh from their repositioning as The Remain Party and conscious that Tory voters on the left and Labour voters on the right are reasonably in their sights; Swinson's intention to 'stop Brexit' may be refreshingly honest – most politicians hide behind the Second Referendum smokescreen – but the leader of a party with 'Democratic' in its name declaring her determination to overturn a democratic mandate has all the undemocratic irony of the world's most totalitarian regimes ruling countries that also boast 'Democratic' as part of their title.

At least Remoaners have a Party leader they can flock to now, anyway; threats of a 'No Deal' Halloween are causing a fair few sleepless nights, I should imagine. Yes, it goes without saying that much amusement has been had via the Woke brigade's tearful tantrums in response to Boris's upgrade; it's always entertaining to see them sob. But it's as much a depressing sign of the times that a dick like Boris Johnson is the best the other side can rally round simply because he winds up the enemy as it is to have Katie Hopkins sold as a champion of free speech. We should be able to do better, but we can't. Oh, well. At least it won't be boring.

CAREFUL WITH THAT AXE, BORIS
25 July 2019

It's funny, but 2016 already seems like a long time ago –
much further back in time than a mere three years, anyway.
Yesterday, I skimmed through a few posts on here from the
moment at which Theresa May moved into Downing Street
and there was mention of her mini-'Night of The Long
Knives' reshuffle. I can barely even remember that now, but
there it was in black-and-white, describing how the post-
Cameron clear-out of the Cabinet saw P45s handed to the
likes of Dave stalwarts Osborne, Gove, Morgan and
Whittingdale; yes, the last name has all-but vanished from
memory, though I seem to recall talk of liaisons with an
'escort' making the headlines at some point. Perhaps the fact
that Mrs May fired a few Ministers when she grabbed the
poisoned chalice has been utterly forgotten due to the record
number that left of their own volition during her brief tenure
in office; some of them have now come in from the cold at the
behest of Boris.

Following the now-customary exercise in sentimental
insincerity that accompanies the farewell performance of a
Prime Minister at the dispatch-box, Mrs May was swiftly
dispatched to the past tense by her successor – as were most
of her Ministers. The speed that the new PM employed was
undoubtedly necessary; after all, he only has 99 days to keep
his most important promise; but the scale of the 'massacre'
perhaps reflected the urgency he exhibited during his rapid-
fire inaugural address before the press yesterday afternoon.
He doesn't have the luxury of test-driving Ministers with L-
plates; it makes much more sense to assemble essentially the
same 'Team Boris' he would have put together three years
ago had his anticipated coronation not been postponed and
he'd had a little more breathing space than he has now.

Some of the most inflexible Remainers – Hammond, Stewart, Lidington, Gauke – walked the plank voluntarily, whereas Jeremy (he's an entrepreneur) Hunt decided to jump rather than face demotion. All would have been obstructive obstacles to Johnson's intentions, yet a notable Brexiteer such as Penny Mordaunt has also been shown the door, presumably because she supported Hunt in the leadership contest. One of the first to sign-up to the Leave side in 2016, the incomparably incompetent Chris Grayling, has gone too – though I was quite looking forward to seeing which Ministry he'd be let loose on next. Plenty of Ministers whose names are so forgettable that their faces are impossible to evoke have been axed as well, the kind like Northern Ireland Secretary Karen Bradley or Culture and Digital Minister Jeremy Wright (no, me neither), whose lack of interest in (or qualification for) the posts they were awarded mirrored the cluelessness of the woman who awarded them.

Back in March, the avalanche of resignations left 15 ministerial posts vacant; it began to look like either nobody wanted them or the dearth of talent within the Conservative Party meant there was nobody to fill them. The return of Amber Rudd to the Cabinet, a year after the former Home Secretary had been forced to carry the can for Windrush policies instigated by Mrs May, highlighted the PM's desperation. Now Rudd is one of the few survivors of the cull, having shrewdly amended her opposition to the No Deal option. She breathes a sigh of relief alongside Sajid Javid, Michael Gove, Liz Truss and Matt Hancock. Amongst the notable returning ex-Ministers are Priti Patel, Dominic Raab, Andrea Leadsom, Esther McVey, Nicky Morgan, Theresa Villiers, and that crafty Gavin Williamson, creeping back in with the stealth of a certain tarantula after a mere 84 days in the sin bin. Brother Jo is back too.

Swapping the Home Office for the Treasury is not the most optimistic of moves when one is made aware of Sajid Javid's somewhat questionable grasp of figures. In his senior managerial role at Deutsche Bank before he entered Parliament, Javid enthusiastically embraced a tax-avoidance scheme that resulted in a courtroom defeat when it was exposed; as Business Secretary, he ended the Business Growth Service, a much-needed and profitable sponsor of small businesses; and he also gave the green light to the sale of Tata Steel's Scunthorpe branch to a company with a disastrous track record, a company which upheld its reputation with the swift slide of British Steel into administration. Let's hope he remembers to pack his calculator when he moves in to No.11. Like the resurfacing of Priti Patel's previous (?) views on capital punishment now that she has been promoted to Home Secretary, Javid's present will inevitably be viewed through the prism of his past if he buggers it up.

Ironically, for all the talk of the hard right and its rigid racial/social elitism having seized control, some have pointed out the accidental 'multicultural mix' at the very tip of the Tory iceberg. On Twitter, journalist Tom Harwood asked if this was the most 'Woke' the four great offices of state have ever been – 'The grandson of a Turkish Muslim, the daughter of Indian-Ugandan Hindus, the son of Pakistani Muslims, and the son of a Jewish Czech refugee.' Or is this backdoor diversity, achieved organically and without any inclusivity committees, shortlists and affirmative-action initiatives? Of course, the ethnic origins of those mentioned should be irrelevant to the skills required for the job, but it's not difficult to imagine how the Labour Party would have made something of a song-and-dance about having a 'Diversity Cabinet' and milked it to the max.

The Ministers May fired in 2016 were expected to be troublesome from the backbenches, though Mrs May found those actually in the Cabinet (certainly after 2017) far more troublesome than the odd Rees-Mogg outside the tent pissing-in. But May's concerns were initially eased by the fact she inherited a working majority from her predecessor; the same does not apply for Boris. If the Tories lose the upcoming Brecon and Radnorshire by-election to the Lib Dems, Johnson's majority will be reduced to two. There's no doubt the absence of time before a certain deadline has prompted the new PM into acting with such ruthless swiftness, but I suspect a motion of no confidence emanating from a Labour-Lib Dem alliance will only come when/if a package from Brussels sprouts before the Commons. However, if the Tory 'rebels' will be sufficiently irked at losing their jobs and sufficiently dedicated to the Remain agenda to vote down their own Government, the General Election to follow could well make real their recurring nightmare of a Corbyn administration. We shall see.

This week's heat-wave may not last as long as the dry spell that made last summer so uncomfortable for those of us averse to a tropical climate, but I've a feeling the temperature will remain extremely high in Westminster until the autumn. Boris knows he has to deliver and deliver fast. If he's to avoid presiding over the shortest tenure at No.10 in history, he needs to keep the knotted hanky mothballed and work through the holiday season. He's made a start.

DON'T PANIC!
30 July 2019

'...since the war' was once the most overused barometer for measuring a crisis; you couldn't avoid it when I was a kid in the 1970s – though considering anyone older than, say, 35 back then would have had a first-hand memory of some aspect of the conflict, perhaps it's no surprise it was the suffix of choice. Watch archive BBC coverage of the February 1974 General Election and the phrase peppers the programme; but one has a real sense of what prompted its recurrence when even revellers in Trafalgar Square watching the results come in are forced to do so in the dark. 'The gravest economic crisis since the war' is the context, though one wonders how many times that particular expression had been uttered by opportunistic politicians in the 29 years following VE Day.

The winter of 1946/47 produced *literally* the gravest economic crisis since the war – or at least the first such one experienced. Retrospectively relegated to a footnote when the far more celebrated 1962/63 cold spell is recalled, the chill that descended upon the British Isles in January 1947 was equally devastating. In some respects, its impact was even greater than the winter of 16 years later in that it stretched the limited resources of a country already struggling through a protracted recovery from the battering it had taken on the home front. The Arctic temperatures wiped out a quarter of the nation's sheep, decimated up to 20% of crops and were responsible for industrial production falling 10%. The standing of Attlee's Labour Government plummeted as fuel stocks and food supplies dwindled in the big freeze, with imposed emergency measures having a seismic effect on morale; the floods that came with the March thaw were an additional blow to a beleaguered Britain.

When another Labour Government 20 years later dithered and delayed before belatedly devaluing the pound – at a time when such an action was viewed as a national humiliation – the chaos that cost Jim Callaghan his tenancy of No.11 Downing Street and fatally damaged the Wilson administration was regarded as...'the gravest economic crisis since the war'. Yet Wilson's immediate Conservative successor came a cropper within three-and-a-half years of redecorating No.10, as quadrupling oil prices exploited by the key-holders of the country's prime fuel supply – the miners – panicked Ted Heath into switching out the lights and passing round the candles. At the time, I remember asking my dad why the Germans were richer than us when they'd lost the war. This was when I found out parents don't have all the answers.

Where Heath's Tories had failed, Labour – under Wilson and then Callaghan – soldiered on in impossible circumstances, but still had to suffer the shame of crawling cap-in-hand to the IMF in 1976. Less than three years later, the unions 'Sunny Jim' had always been able to depend upon bit the hand that fed them because they had acquired the appetite of Oliver Twist. Another terrible winter – this time of Discontent – handed electoral victory to Margaret Thatcher as we once again endured 'the gravest economic crisis since the war'. I have vivid memories of that winter, and as even the all-powerful omnipotence of television joined the catalogue of public services falling into stasis like donkey-jacketed dominos, the palpable feeling of imminent collapse made an impression that I've tended to view subsequent crises through the prism of. As a consequence, they rarely measure up and I tend to take Lance Corporal Jones's advice.

It was almost 30 years before we encountered a comparable crisis – though even the Credit Crunch and the severe Austerity measures introduced by the Coalition in 2010 didn't induce the same sense of being on the brink as 1978/79 did. The situation may have claimed the scalp of yet another Labour Government and exacerbated the schism between the haves and the have-nots, but the 2010-2015 Con-Dem regime acted like a ruthless receiver dividing the assets of an insolvent company. The climate was not one of the country being ungovernable or out of control. It took the unexpected outcome of a certain unnecessary referendum to finally return us to the state of existential emergency that provoked the return of '...since the war'.

It's interesting that the most hysterical reactions to the result of the 2016 EU Referendum emanated largely from those born and raised in the 1990s and early 2000s, a period now regarded as a rare oasis of economic calm – strong and stable, one might say. And that's not merely the general public; many children of Blair whose degrees in Media Studies facilitated their rises through the broadcasting and print medium ranks were similarly green when it came to a crisis and responded to a scenario for which they hadn't been prepared in a fittingly OTT manner that has spiralled out of all proportion over the last three years. 'Crashing out of the EU', 'stolen my future' and 'staring into the abyss' have joined '...since the war' in the Remainer lexicon; but WWII has also been revived as an unlikely yardstick by the other side, with 'Dunkirk Spirit' and misplaced allusions to Churchill making a comeback, even though (unlike the 1970s) they are being evoked by those who may as well talk of Trafalgar or Waterloo for all the relevance they have to their own experience.

Maybe a generation or two subconsciously yearned to have their malnourished mettle tested by a crisis. There's an almost masochistic relish in fantasising about apocalyptic scenarios of the kind George Osborne forecasted on the eve of the Referendum, and the prospect of No Deal seems to have 'turbo-charged' (© every f***ing Boris Minister) the nightmarish imagery, fetishising the vision of empty supermarket shelves, bare chemist's cupboards, martial law and primeval anarchy. Perhaps sitting through more zombie movies and games than is advisable has convinced some too young to know any better that a crisis only has the one outcome.

However, if history has taught us anything it is that crises are no more permanent than their polar opposite; no boom without bust and vice-versa. The wars Brits have been engaged in since 1945 have all taken place in far-flung locations, giving non-combatants an abstract perspective on conflict that doctored news reports from distant war-zones seem to have played their part in. Domestic *economic* crises, on the other hand, impinge upon our lives in ways that personalise their offensiveness and amplify their impact. But the genuine crisis in so many of our public services, for example, has bugger-all to do with Brexit; they're in a bad way because they've been under-funded for decades, and the blame is with the Remainer village of Westminster, not the rest of Brexit Britain.

When it comes to a crisis, it's probably best not to hang on every word of that metropolitan Mother Shipton, Emily Maitlis – the Remoaner Lord Haw-Haw issuing proclamations of doom 'n' gloom on a nightly basis. Many of us have experienced personal crises that have hit us at times when the nation had allegedly never had it so good, and the state of the nation has had no bearing on mine at all; the damage was restricted to the smallest of circles rather than the widest of canvasses. External events might occasionally contribute to the picture, but whether we find ourselves in the Promised Land or downtown Dystopia on 1 November, the nation will keep buggering on and so will we. However bad it gets, it then gets better - always.

THE FEAR
3 August 2019

I remember a first date once, which – though an encouraging start – turned out to be merely the prologue to another example of why my being one half of 'a lovely couple' is the relationship equivalent of a coalition government, i.e. an exceedingly rare aberration destined to end in tears. But I was younger at the time, so can be excused. And, anyway, she was a fascinating woman who worked for a charity and was about to jet off on a related business trip to New York. A second date was definitely on the cards, but the Manhattan outing would put it back a week or two. I resolved to pick up some kind of quirky guide to the Big Apple for her and pass it on before she packed her suitcase.

One topic of conversation that came up during the evening was a shared recollection of early 80s nuclear paranoia. She and I recalled the collective fear of those years, when pre-apocalypse tension infected the culture and seemed doomed to become a self-fulfilling prophesy; it was the age of Greenham Common, 'Threads' and 'Two Tribes'. My date and I agreed such a bleak atmosphere genuinely (and thankfully) appeared to be a thing of the past – at least where the west was concerned. And when, you may ask, did this rather pleasant exchange take place? Why, to be exact, September 10 2001.

I was in a second-hand bookshop the following day when, having located just the kind of offbeat volume I'd intended, I heard something strange was happening at the World Trade Centre; the shopkeeper shrewdly informed me a fire in one of the twin towers had sent it crashing to the ground only after I'd bought the bloody book. Of course, it was no use to its recipient, as the trip to New York was cancelled and the state of global emergency she and I had perhaps unwisely relegated to the past tense suddenly re-emerged uglier than ever in the here and now. And, although the panic 9/11 unleashed unsurprisingly lasted longer than my dalliance with this particular lady, the numerous offshoots of the September 11 attacks that are still with us have sadly become part of the cultural wallpaper.

I don't know if it's fair to say that those of us who were transfixed by the grotesque sights on our TV screens 18 years ago have gradually become immune to the horrors embodied in the events of 9/11 since. But exposure to subsequent wars and terrorist atrocities with their roots in that day could possibly have engendered a subliminal immunity so that what initially provoked genuine fear of a potential WWIII scenario is now met with shoulder-shrugging weariness. During the recent blanket coverage of the first Moon Landing's 50th anniversary, one overlooked fact left out of the celebrations was that the viewing public of the time became bored with the great adventure so quickly that the only other Apollo mission anyone ever recalls is 13 – and that crew never even made it to their destination. When an achievement as immense as men on the moon can induce a jaded response as one lunar landing rapidly follows another, perhaps the repeated detonation of bombs in a crowded environment fails to maintain the level of shock such an appalling act warrants simply because it's just one more atrocity in a very long line of them.

The world is far more intricately connected today than it was in 2001 – a period when social media was in its infancy and traditional mediums still had a monopoly on the way we consumed news. Indeed, the only occasion in which I can ever remember the newspaper racks being emptied in my local supermarket was the day after 9/11; everybody had clearly purchased a paper as a souvenir, just as their fathers (or grandfathers) had when Kennedy was assassinated in 1963.

It's hard to imagine that happening with an equivalent incident today. I suspect many a website or search engine would crash, but there'd still be plenty of Fleet Street's finest waiting to find a home. Then again, how long would shock linger now? Long enough for that interminable 24 hours between a story breaking and it making the physical front page? Probably not. The nature of how news is transmitted to the masses has changed so much since 2001 that the manner of its digestion has changed too – as has its presentation, presumably in order to hold the diminishing attention span of the reader. Often it seems that stories which don't really deserve the dramatic headline ape the major event so that each and every item battling for space has to be given the full (to use a quaint old phrase) 'stop press' treatment.

It could be a result of living through two traumatic post-9/11 decades or it could simply be my age, but I find I don't lose sleep over any of the news stories designed to provoke panic nowadays. I feel almost ashamed to admit it, for I realise I'm supposed to be in a perpetual state of fear – fear of climate change or Brexit or knife-crime or the far-right or the far-left or Boris or Corbyn or Trump or Putin or China or North Korea or No Deal...and yet, I'm not. However, that's not to say I don't *care;* caring about an important issue and (on occasion) being passionate about a few is listed on my membership card of the human race – and I hope that's been evident in some of the things I've written here. But I don't worry about today's shock-horror stories, certainly not the level of worry I'm constantly told I should feel. Then again, being told how I should feel is something that media in all its current incarnations has come to specialise in.

Media of the social variety is regularly – and often rightly – castigated for its 'echo chamber' tendencies, and (should I wish to do so) I can certainly think of an easy way in which I could severely deplete my friends list on Facebook overnight, simply by expressing an opinion I'm not supposed to possess, let alone express. But hasn't the new media merely learnt the lessons of the old media? Yes, Facebook and Twitter reflect users' already established opinions back at them, confirming biases and upholding prejudices whilst discouraging discovering different perspectives; but then again, so do the Daily Mail and the Guardian. This trend could also be responsible for the current vogue in looking at an unfavourable event from a favourable angle in order to make it more palatable to those it upsets.

The remarkable success of the Brexit Party in the recent European Elections was countered by its opponents combining the split Remain vote as spurious evidence that Nigel's barmy army didn't actually win after all. The same tactic was applied in the wake of the Brecon & Radnorshire by-election by the other side, showing how putting the Tory and Brexit Party votes together somehow proved the Lib Dems were actually the losers. The fact that none of these combinations actually appeared as such on the ballot paper is regarded as almost immaterial when it comes to a 'moral victory' – or it could just be that this curious development proves how the Remainer/Leaver divide now counts for more than traditional party allegiances.

I considered using Nick Ross's sage advice as the title for this post, and then remembered I'd used it as the title of an obituary for 'Crimewatch' I penned on here whenever it was that the show ended its lengthy run. As a matter of fact, I *do* have nightmares – constantly; and they're horrible, far worse than any I had as a kid. But they're all of a domestic nature, nocturnal kitchen-sink dramas featuring those I have loved and those I have lost; they don't contain any bogeymen that dominate national or international headlines at all. Perhaps it's because I'm in a strange place that I don't scare easily anymore – at least when I'm awake.

NOT MY PRIME MINISTER
14 August 2019

As someone currently in the thick of manic creative hysteria – don't think that's a recognised syndrome, but it should be – I can sympathise with the increasingly-detached-from-reality mania afflicting the Remainer majority at Westminster; well, to a point. My own experience is of hammering at this bloody keyboard for hours at a time, desperately trying to transcribe the relentless flow of words pouring out of my fevered head with the same speed they appear in it; even when I take a break and try to unwind with brown bread and eggs (hearty meals not being conducive to the condition), I have a notepad beside me, for I cannot switch off. I've been like this for about a fortnight now, and it's exhausting as well as mind-altering. You really do inhabit a world of your own making, one in which normal rules do not apply. It would seem I'm not alone.

Over the last three years, attempts to overturn the result of the 2016 EU Referendum by the losing side have gone from street protest to Project Fear to Second Referendum to where we are now, a new video game called 'Fantasy Prime Minister'. In this, the player gets to choose which MP he or she would rather have in 10 Downing Street than the man who's been there for less than a month. The player can pick from the incumbent Leader of the Opposition ol' Jezza or the Lib Dem leader Jo Swinson; they can pick the sole Green in the team, Caroline Lucas; or they can even opt for a couple of veterans who were never elected leaders of their respective parties, Ken Clarke and Harriet Harman. Once a prospective PM is selected, the player then engages in a series of gripping constitutional crises, battling for the right to replace an unelected premier with an unelected premier.

In order to derail what appears to be a determined No Deal 'crashing out' (© 'Newsnight') policy being pursued by Boris and the Brexiteers (great Merseybeat band name), Remainers have this week scaled unprecedented peaks of foaming-at-the-mouth fantasies they seriously believe will rescue us from ruin in the event of Boris being defeated in an expected no confidence vote. A Government of National Unity is one phrase we've heard a lot, but a country as disunited as ours currently is means such an administration would require representation from both ends of the great divide to truly unify; and nobody proposing the National Unity concept is proposing that. A Government of Remain Unity would be more accurate. When Caroline Lucas put forward her amusing idea of a middle-class 'mumsnet' Cabinet led by her in full headmistress mode, the only issue her side of the divide took with the notion was the absence of 'women of colour' from the line-up. The mind-boggling undemocratic ludicrousness of the proposal wasn't a problem, apparently.

National Unity was much-discussed in the inconclusive wake of the February 1974 General Election, but Ted Heath's proposals for coalition with Jeremy Thorpe's Liberals floundered and Harold Wilson led Labour back to power with a minority administration. An actual peacetime 'National' Government comprising members from all three major parties had, of course, existed from 1931 until the outbreak of the Second World War; and though initially led by Labour's Ramsay MacDonald, it was overwhelmingly Tory-dominated, as would've been any Heath/Thorpe coalition in 1974 and as indeed was the coalition led by Lloyd George in the aftermath of WWI. We don't even have to go back that far to discern the imbalance in most coalition administrations and how the ultimate aim is more a case of the largest party keeping out the opposition rather than any noble aspiration to save the nation.

Jeremy Corbyn's brainwave of playing the part of a caretaker PM to prevent the Halloween deadline coming to pass before then calling a General Election which he assumes he will win is bonkers, but at least he *is* the leader of the second largest party in the Commons. He is, however, dependent on disgruntled Tory backbenchers to achieve this aim, and while Enoch Powell may have advocated voting Labour in 1974, today's Remainer Tories feel this is a rebellion too far.

Anyway, Jezza's own ambiguous stance on the EU has been a hindrance to any successful exploitation by Labour of the Conservative divisions over the issue, and this clearly rankles with Jo Swinson, who doesn't seem keen on the prospect of Corbyn at No.10, even if it means another Brexit delay is more likely. But then, the Lib Dem leader has been quite brazen that it's her intention to prevent Brexit altogether, so merely kicking the date we leave back into the long grass yet again just isn't good enough. The notion of giving the gig to Clarke or Harman is seen by Swinson as a genuinely realistic alternative to Corbyn. I mean, yes, good old Ken is the Father of the House and everyone's favourite jazz-loving, hush puppy-wearing Tory uncle; but get real. As for Ms Harperson – come on!

But this is where we are. So intense is the panic amongst the hardcore Remainers now, nothing is deemed too fantastical. Caroline Lucas included Nicola Sturgeon in her fantasy Cabinet, and the First Minister isn't even an MP. Why stop at nominating a prominent Remainer who at least happens to be a politician (albeit in the wrong parliament), though? Why not send out the call to Gary Lineker? Brian Cox? Greta

Thunberg? And, no doubt, Chuka Umunna would be up for it too – how many parties has he been a member of this year? Anyway, this dream Guardian Government would revoke Article 50, reverse the Referendum result and deliver the same kind of 'fuck you' to 17 million members of the electorate as they themselves received three years ago. Lest we forget, the electorate will have no say at all – just as they didn't when Boris succeeded Theresa. Why let such unnecessary annoyances like the electorate get in the way of democracy, though?

Considering we're marking the 200th anniversary of the Peterloo Massacre this week – an event regarded as a watershed moment on the long and winding road to universal suffrage – it's ironic that we're currently watching politicians attempting to seize power (or hold onto it) without any involvement from voters at all. With the Government reduced to a majority of one, of course, it's inevitable we'll see a General Election before the scheduled date of 2022, probably before the end of this year; but what happens in the months leading up to the hustings appears to be being scripted by Chris Morris. I might regard myself as a bit fanatical at the moment – and if anyone could observe me during this breathless creative process they'd probably conclude I'm a bit 'frazzled'. Compared to that lot down Westminster way, however, I feel confident I'd receive a clean bill of health. If I could get an appointment at my local GPs surgery, of course. Which, needless to say, I can't. Welcome to 2019. It's mad.

THE DAY WAR BROKE OUT
29 August 2019

There have been a lot of Twitter knickers in a twist over the past 48 hours; then again, it's hard to think of a time when there aren't. The globe's favourite social media platform for the outraged and offended has rarely observed such a thing as a Sabbath, and the polarising political climate in Britain since June 2016 has seen Twitter established as the battleground that never sleeps. Every development instigated by one side of the Brexit divide is fought at its most furious by the other not in the Commons, but in cyberspace; and after Tuesday's coming together of Remainer MPs – despite the amusingly delusional Jo Swinson's refusal to accept the candidacy of the Leader of the Opposition in the event of one unelected PM usurping another – the bursting of their bubble by Boris 24 hours later sent melodramatic hysteria into unmissable overdrive.

First of all, there was Brexiteer outrage at Remainer attempts to sabotage democracy as an effective Second Referendum/Revoke Article 50/Scrap Brexit coalition belatedly emerged; then there was Remainer outrage at Brexiteer attempts to sabotage democracy by proroguing Parliament and denying debate on the issue until there's not enough time left to stop the No Deal Apocalypse. Both opposing parties are claiming 'The People' as their own, even though the people in question are merely those on *their* respective sides of the barricades; those who voted the wrong way can go whistle or at least submit to a course of re-education to understand why they're in the wrong and the other side is in the right. Over three years on, and Cameron's toxic legacy is more divisive than ever; indeed, it's hard to see any potential resolution between the warring factions at all. A shame Ian Paisley and Martin McGuinness are no longer around to bring everyone together.

However, thank God so many of the entitled egomaniacs fuelling the divisions remain oblivious to how stupid (and inadvertently entertaining) they are. Paul Mason played a manic street preacher preaching to the converted in a video aired on 'Newsnight' before appearing in the studio, predicting Poll Tax Riots-style civil unrest as the inevitable outcome if his side don't get their way; and this after his side have constantly decried the other side for intimidating Remainer MPs outside Parliament, as though the other side's notion of expressing their democratic right to protest somehow lacks the 'purity' of his side's right to do likewise. To emphasise his working-class credentials, Mason invoked the fighting spirit of his hometown Leigh, conveniently overlooking the fact that the Metropolitan Borough of Wigan (to which Leigh belongs) voted 63.9 % Leave in 2016; but maybe Leigh has suffered the same post-industrial dismissal by the political class – the one that Mason's attitude upholds – as neighbouring Bury; no wonder such places remain defined by what little they have left, like their football clubs...

John McDonnell, a man whose approach to taking on his opponents is juvenile at best, was also on hand with the microphone at the impromptu alfresco shindig in the wake of yesterday's Downing Street announcement, as was Diane 'abacus' Abbott and Keir 'Plastic Man' Starmer. Nobody present could be left in any doubt that those who have facilitated the longest unbroken Parliamentary session since the Civil War are outraged. Such outrage was noticeably absent from the Remoaner camp when an electronically-tagged convicted criminal who just happened to be a Labour MP played her part in disrupting democracy by casting the decisive vote a few months ago, of course, and what of Mr Speaker himself? Little John has hardly been a bastion of impartiality, has he? But it's okay 'cause *he's one of us*. The hypocrisy is hilarious.

I should imagine the PM probably had the proroguing plan ready and waiting for the right moment and he certainly seems to have timed it to perfection, ensuring Brenda's seal of approval just one day after the parade of smug, holier-than-thou signatories to Jezza's proposal queued-up on camera to sing from a shared hymn sheet at last, united in their righteous conviction. When the other side try to enact the will of the majority, that other side divides; when *they* try to enact the will of the minority, they unify; when the other side tries to prevent those responsible for blocking a democratic decision for three years from continuing to do so, it's a coup; when *they* attempt to put together a fantasy 'Caretaker Government' of hand-picked losers for the purpose of reversing that democratic decision, they're saving the nation.

It's handy that we're on the eve of the 80th anniversary of Mr Chamberlain's declaration of war, for the tireless and tedious evocation of 'fighting them on the beaches' by Brexiteers not even old enough to have been Mods or Rockers in the 60s is a baton that has now been grabbed by the other side. After rightly ridiculing the irrelevant summoning of the Dunkirk Spirit by their opponents, some prominent Remoaners have once again decided when they do the same thing it's not the same at all. 'You will not destroy the freedoms my grandfather fought two world wars to defend' tweeted Hugh Grant – not from beaches littered with bodies; 'Weep for Britain. A sick, cynical and brutal and horribly dangerous coup d'état' added Stephen Fry – not from a dead and long-abandoned Lancashire mill-town.

Perish the thought that politicians might be motivated by cynical self-interest, of course; the possibility Boris Johnson could be seeking to hold onto his job via his recent actions is as appalling as the possibility Jeremy Corbyn could be seeking to steal it via *his* recent actions. No, as ever, the moral high-ground is always with whichever guys you have decided are the good ones.

A three-week suspension of Parliament by the PM is standard procedure in the early autumn, allowing the party conference season to progress free from its star performers being recalled to Westminster for an emergency vote; adding a couple of weeks to the usual break is not really surprising considering the circumstances. Neither is the fact that by doing so, all those who endorse the decision are going back on what they'd said on the subject just a few weeks or tweets ago. They're being led by Boris Johnson, don't forget. After imagining they'd pulled a master-stroke in managing to temporarily gather all No Deal opponents under one united umbrella, the Remainer brigade are now confronted by the inevitable fact they have even less time to finally kill a democratic mandate than they thought. No wonder they're upset. They're going to take it to the streets, apparently; I wonder if Jon Snow will be on hand to count the number of non-white faces when they do.

TO BE CONTINUED
5 September 2019

'They won't let it happen, y'know' – so spoke a shrewd Leave-voting friend of mine two years ago, back when the farce to block Brexit was barely twelve months into its record-breaking run. I doubted her word then; I doubt it no longer. Yes, we've all come a long way since 2017, let alone 2016. And this week has seen such an action-packed chapter in the saga that it's something of a challenge to issue this brief summary of events as an up-to-date bulletin because it'll probably be superseded by other events by the time it appears. From what I can work out at the moment, Boris Johnson has offered the Labour Party precisely what they most desire on a plate – but will they take the bait? This is like Tom popping a slab of cheese before Jerry's hole-in-the-wall, and Jerry wrestling with the demands of his appetite, knowing from the off that his feline nemesis has set yet another trap.

99

So, the most vocal Second Referendum proponents won't consent to a genuine 'People's Vote' after all; no, they won't let the electorate have their say if there's a risk that by doing so they themselves might lose their seats. Jo Swinson has gone on the record that she won't accept the result of another referendum if it ends up being the result she doesn't want, anyway, so why should we be surprised by this latest surreal development? The Fixed Term Parliaments Act, one more contributing factor towards David Cameron's candidacy as the Prime Minister with the most damaging legacy on record, is an irrelevant encumbrance to getting things done that should have been repealed the second the Coalition ceased to be. It is entirely responsible for yet another impasse when the loss of the Government's tiny numerical advantage over its opponents demands the traditional resolution.

We now have the bizarre situation whereby a Prime Minister without a majority has to go cap-in-hand to a hostile Commons, seeking permission to dissolve Parliament – and being refused permission. Of course, Boris's motivation for doing so is not quite black-and-white (to put it mildly); but the power to call a General Election without recourse to Parliament should never have been stripped from the resident of No.10 – especially when we currently have a Parliament that cannot agree on anything. Well, a majority can agree on *something,* and that will be demonstrated when the bill to block a no-deal Brexit is fast-tracked through the tortoise marathon of the Lords.

Another episode in this gripping chapter came with the 21 expulsions from the Conservative Party – numerous grandees (including the Father of the House himself) and recent Cabinet Ministers all deselected overnight, rebranded as Independents and prevented from standing as Tories ever again; never before has rebellion against one's own party been so ruthlessly punished. Boris's own brother Jo, a serial quitter – how many times has he walked out of the Cabinet now? – has resigned as an MP today, adding further minus marks against this administration's numbers; the PM has already experienced the choreographed stunt of a dishonourable member crossing the floor of the House in the middle of a speech this week; and while the instant dismissal of the 21 rebels may have been a promised reprisal the Prime Minister was faced with no alternative but to carry out, the authority to govern based on a greater proportion of seats has been completely obliterated now. No Government in living memory has ever been so swiftly diminished, and yet for the electorate to be denied their say as a consequence seems to be one more example of the elected's blatant contempt for those who elect them.

The sole beneficiaries of the crises eating away at the heart of both the Conservative and Labour Parties are the Lib Dems; having gained a Tory this week, Swinson and her anti-democratic cronies have now secured a former Labour member, albeit one who took the Umunna route from Labour to TIG to CHUK to Lib Dem. Luciana Berger famously quit Labour after well-documented and sustained anti-Semitic abuse, so her decision to walk seemed to be more understandable and worthy of sympathy than some of the colleagues who followed in her wake. But it appears the Lib Dems are now very much the Battersea Dog's Home for MPs unloved and unwanted by their own parties; the fact that many of them represent Leave-voting constituencies is pure coincidence, of course. No wonder Jo Swinson is so against a snap Election when the sudden boost to her number of seats could be wiped out all over again if the polling stations are reopened for business tomorrow.

Justine Greening, Education Secretary for a while under Theresa May, announced a couple of days ago that she won't be defecting to the Lib Dems, but will stand down altogether; possibly jumping before she's pushed, yes, though it's a sign of these turbulent times that Tory MPs who would previously have been regarded as future prospects with plenty more to offer are deciding their party is no longer conducive to their worldview. The cliché often trotted out about the Conservative or Labour Parties being 'broad churches' capable of encompassing a variety of opinions appears to be utterly redundant now.

Reluctant as I am to agree with the Lord of Darkness Peter Mandelson, I actually thought he had a fair point when he reminded people how Tony Blair never expelled Jeremy Corbyn from the Labour Party despite Jezza's serial rebellions when in his backbench comfort zone; today, whether Labour or Tory, so narrow has the focus of the leadership and the leader's advisers become that any deviation from the script will not be tolerated. In the end, it is the two parties themselves – whether represented by Labour's Momentum takeover or the Tories' capitulation to the ERG – that will suffer as both begin to resemble single issue pressure groups rather than wide collectives capable of addressing *all* the problems that need sorting instead of just the ones reflecting the interests of the elites at the pinnacle of the pyramid.

So, Boris will apparently put the call for a General Election to the Commons again on Monday, following the anticipated assimilation into law of the bill to block a no-deal Brexit. The majority of Labour's leading lights want to hold back an Election until yet one more extension to D-Day has been secured, thus preventing Boris from repealing no-deal legislation. That's what they say, anyway. More than three years after the event, we are where we are because they actually don't want to do what the majority told them to do; and for all her faults, at least Jo Swinson is being honest. Maybe they *won't* let it happen, y'know.

PROROGUE STATE
10 September 2019

A mate of mine recently indulged in a bit of cash-in-hand work roadying for – wait for it – ye olde Goth band Fields of the Nephilim (yes, they still exist); for those who weren't regular readers of the music press in the mid-80s, the Nephilim were the Boyzone to The Sisters of Mercy's Take That. Never major league players, the band nevertheless continue to attract a committed cult of hardcore followers on the road, some of whom have clearly experienced mental health issues according to the reports I received of the ones camped outside every venue on the tour. Acting as a makeshift security guard to keep said fans away from the band, my friend exchanged a few civil words with them and was a little unnerved by their stalker-like, delusional conviction they were on intimate terms with individual members; if they could just say hello, all would be well with the world.

I only thought of this because I noticed those bloody flags being waved once again outside Parliament yesterday; the brandishers of both EU and Union Jack varieties are now a seemingly permanent fixture whenever a live broadcast takes place from Westminster – and there have been plenty of those of late. The same old shouting in an attempt to drown out updates on Commons events has become a tedious accompaniment to the sight of the flags themselves. Yes, this is an issue that provokes passions (which is putting it mildly), but to be there apparently every day all day long takes either incredible stamina or simply reflects the same absence of any other purpose in life as evident in the Nephilim stalkers. At least that guy who set up a 'peace camp' on Parliament Square and lived in a tent there for years appeared quite chilled-out; this lot seem to be akin to noisy neighbours engaged in a never-ending back-garden barbeque.

Within the walls of the establishment they're intent on besieging, behaviour was rather less dignified, however; and it started as it meant to go on. Confronted by the unprecedented protocol-breaking threat of the Tories planning to put forward a candidate to stand against the Speaker (still a member of their own party) at the next Election, Bercow bowed-out at last – or at least announced the date of his departure. The fact he chose 31 October was entirely in keeping with the relentless exhibitionism of his ego, eager to steal the headlines on a day he knew even the dependable vanity of his puffed-up posturing might not be enough to make him the centre of attention.

What followed Bercow's announcement – delivered in the curious manner of an Englishman abroad trying to make himself understood to a native – was a nauseating outpouring of sentimental arse-licking listing the Speaker's achievements in the chair, albeit praise that mysteriously overlooked recent bullying allegations or even Bercow's membership of the horrible pro-Apartheid Monday Club back in his Young Conservative days. The standing ovation Little John received from the Opposition side of the House was in stark contrast to the sedentary reaction from the Government side, though both were equally stage-managed with all the childish petulance we've sadly come to expect from the tenants of this particular Palace.

But, of course, despite Bercow's desperation to be the lead story on the bulletins, the latest instalment in the exciting adventures of Boris the Prime Minister inevitably claimed top-of-the-bill status when the time came for debate. The resignation of Amber Rudd over the weekend has been portrayed by some as a catastrophic blow to the Government, yet her presence as a prominent Remainer in the PM's Cabinet seemed incongruous from the off, especially when there was no room for a vocal Brexiteer like Penny Mordaunt. Rudd attempted to justify her survivor status as one of the few leftovers from the Maybot's lot by claiming she had been converted to No Deal as an option, though few were convinced; she cited the expulsion of 21 colleagues from the party as the main reason for her walking, but her tiny majority at the last General Election suggested she might not be around to hold another Ministry come the next one.

Ah, yes – the next General Election; that was the main issue under the spotlight as Monday evening seamlessly segued into Tuesday morning and the Commons paid no heed to the clock. Considering Boris had begun the day sharing a podium with the Taoiseach over in Dublin, he didn't appear sleep-deprived when stating his case for giving the electorate the opportunity to decide. That the Prime Minister even has to plead for the right of the people to elect or evict their representatives is a farce; that a majority of those elected last time round won't sanction that right does far more to demean the standing of honourable members than the PM proroguing Parliament. The double-standard hypocrisy of Labour, Lib Dem and SNP members in decrying the decision to suspend proceedings whilst simultaneously refusing the electorate the chance to play their democratic part is rich indeed. Fine for the plebs to participate in a bloody referendum – whether on the EU or Scottish Independence (remember – those 'once-in-a-lifetime' opportunities?); but when it comes to determining the futures of their elected representatives, forget it.

The grandstanding stunts the opposition parties engaged in when the time finally came for the Speaker to relocate from one House to the other in the bizarre prorogation ceremony were further unedifying examples of their detachment from the voters. To an outsider following events live on BBC Parliament, their theatrical behaviour added to the surreal spectacle of the obscene, otherworldly bubble these people inhabit once they set foot inside that crumbling Gothic edifice whose decaying fixtures and fittings are more than an apt metaphor for the whole rotten institution. I almost felt I was witnessing a scene from the superb 1972 satirical movie on the madness of the British aristocracy, 'The Ruling Class', when the three wise peers solemnly sat before the gathered executive and officially announced Parliament's slide into suspended animation. It was certainly a viewing experience straight from the imagination of Lewis Carroll, but as a portrait of Great British democracy in 2019, it kind-of said everything.

So, Party Conference season up next, and then we're back in five weeks for the Queen's Speech. Boris and his team will have hoped to have evaded a No Deal grilling by then, despite demands (and apparently legal requirements) for confidential correspondence on 'Project Yellowhammer' to be made public. The PM is insistent he can achieve a deal with the EU before Halloween, but remains adamant he won't beg for yet another extension to the endlessly delayed deadline, regardless of the new law saying he must do so and the additional threat of a possible spell behind bars if he refuses. And even if the postponed General Election Labour have spent the last two years calling for won't sort out a shambles entirely of Parliament's making, it would at least give voters the chance to show the door to so many whose arrogant entitlement and superiority complexes have put us where we are.

2
Those we have loved –
And those we have lost

Pop and the personal

A CLASS ACT
9 February 2019

Swivel-eyed get – what a wonderfully vivid description of an interfering busybody. It gate-crashed the national lexicon when Arthur Seaton was confronted by the actions of 'Old Ma Bull', a characteristic battleaxe familiar to anyone who had grown-up in an immediate post-war working-class community, the kind that would shortly be given iconic properties courtesy of 'Coronation Street', whereby Old Ma Bull would be remade and remodelled as Ena Sharples. The 1960 movie of Alan Sillitoe's 'kitchen-sink' novel, 'Saturday Night and Sunday Morning' laid the ground for Tony Warren's transfer of the Angry Young Man's *oeuvre* from silver to small screen at the end of that year; but Albert Finney's interpretation of the book's lead character has remained a British cinematic touchstone that every anti-hero has followed ever since, even when the actors taking their cue from Finney's pioneering lead don't necessarily recognise the taste of the chip on the character's shoulder.

Albert Finney, Tom Courtenay, Terence Stamp, Michael Caine – actors whose grammar school backgrounds were no impediment to achievement at a unique moment in recent British history, when social mobility was a reality rather than a theory undone by successive government cuts to the Arts in the state sector. The death at the age of 82 of the first of those landmark thespians to break the mould has served to remind us all that it was once possible to rise from the provinces and reach for the stars bereft of nepotism or economic privilege. Despite the fact that this quartet went on to play a wide variety of roles, the seismic impact they made when kicking down the drawing-room doors at the dawn of a decade that briefly redrew the map of possibilities is something all four will forever be associated with.

However, one only has to look at the legacy of 'Saturday Night and Sunday Morning' via the small screen to realise its groundbreaking authenticity has been diluted and all-but obliterated. Today's television demands have transformed Tony Warren's depiction of Salford from a twice-weekly account of events the audience could relate to into a nightly penny-dreadful document of fantastical melodrama whereby sieges, shootings, murders, abortions, rapes, drug and sexual abuse, fires and explosions are the norm, and where infidelity is apparently compulsory. Taking its sensationalistic cue from the likes of 'Eastenders', 'Emmerdale' and 'Hollyoaks', the 2019 landscape of Weatherfield makes Syria seem a preferable destination.

One could say this week's unsurprising (if appalling) statistics on knife-crime have perhaps demonstrated urban society today is a good deal more dangerous than the one Arthur Seaton swaggered his way through on a Saturday night in 1960; and I would imagine the producers and writers of 'Coronation Street' justify their gory stories by claiming they are merely reflecting that danger via the heightened, exaggerated reality of drama. At the same time, such tactics don't so much exaggerate as distort reality, as though the writers scan the worst headlines and then shoehorn them into the script, giving viewers the impression that society is even more violent than it actually is. Pulp novelist Richard Allen sourced his cult series of 70s books on teenage tribes in much the same way.

The criticism of 'Coronation Street' used to be that it was trapped in a nostalgic time-warp, portraying a cosy cobblestone community that had long since vanished beneath the tower-block; the only remnant of this viewpoint in today's version is the fact that every character in a job has a workplace no more than a dozen paces from their front door.

Otherwise, cosy certainly isn't a word that can be applied to 'Coronation Street' in 2019; a solitary street in which virtually every depressing social issue afflicting the nation can be found in action is hardly cosy, though it's not exactly reality either. And one major casualty of this approach is the crucial element of 'Coronation Street' that served to elevate it above the competition for decades, its humour.

Past writers understood the formula that had made the show so successful; Weatherfield was a place where tragedy and comedy sat cheek-by-jowl, as they do in the real world. Yes, there were plenty of dramatic events on 'Coronation Street' during its first half-century, but there was equally just as much witty writing, characterisation and dialogue worthy of the finest sitcom. This was once a balance that worked well, though perhaps having to stretch storylines so thinly across so many episodes a week has now resulted in a desperate increase of the shock-horror plots at the expense of Stan & Hilda-type hi-jinks, something clueless TV executives deem vital in a ratings battle that has actually never been more irrelevant. If 'Coronation Street' remains a mirror on society, anyone looking through that mirror can only come to the conclusion that society is f****d.

If the streets of terraced houses surrounding the old Raleigh factory in Nottingham that Arthur Seaton knew as home hadn't already been wiped from the map, would they too have descended into the same moral cesspit at their Salford contemporary sixty years on? Probably. Whereas the kitchen-sink heroes – Seaton, Billy Liar, Jimmy Porter *et al* – railed against the iniquities of their uninspired inheritance and fought tooth-and-claw to climb their way out, the way in which their grandchildren are depicted for dramatic purposes lacks the one key ingredient that made those early 60s movies so invigorating and uplifting – hope.

One could argue the decline of social mobility means hope is in short supply as it is, so surely drama should reflect that when turning its focus on those at the bottom of the heap. Unfortunately, by doing so it has the habit of making any relatively rare drama set in a working-class community either on TV or at the cinema a pretty despondent experience. Even whenever a non-Estuary English accent is aired on the likes of 'Woman's Hour' today, the listener knows the subject under discussion is bound to be gangs or drugs or sexual abuse or sex trafficking coz that's what them working-classes do, innit.

Finney has died at 82, Courtenay will be the same age at the end of this month; Stamp is 80; Caine is 85. These guys are either gone or getting very old indeed, and we won't see their likes again because the system that enabled them to succeed isn't there anymore. That's why we're inundated with Cumberbatch's, Lewis's and West's; that's not a criticism of Benedict, Damien or Dominic as actors, but they all had advantages that gave them a head start. A kid without those advantages, a kid in possession of a talent with the potential to flower into that of a Finney or a Courtenay, will have doors barred to him as a result and we'll be denied that talent. We could consequently return to the time before Arthur Seaton, whereby ex-public schoolboys will effectively 'black-up' to play working-class characters, and actors with more authentic origins will be reduced to comedy cockneys or daft northerners. And then the bastards will have ground us down after all.

LEFT-FIELD OF EDEN
26 February 2019

After a promising 'anything goes' start that had been the most fruitful flowering on the fascinating post-punk landscape, the soundtrack of the 1980s eventually homogenised into an insufferably bland template that sadly remains the lazy go-to summary of the decade when it comes to second-hand nostalgia. What this invariably tends to do is obscure the variety of individual voices on offer, voices that became all the more invaluable as the 1980s descended into a mainstream maelstrom of big hair, big shoulder pads, and Big Fun.

David Sylvian, Billy Mackenzie, Julian Cope, Marc Almond – all had at one time been 'Smash Hits' cover stars, yet by the middle of the decade they had drifted away from the spotlight to follow their own idiosyncratic paths, happy to take commercial success if it came but not desperate enough to chase it at the expense of their appetite for adventure. In a way, their journeys echoed those of similarly-minded mavericks of the previous decade such as Roy Harper, Richard Thompson, John Martyn and Peter Hammill. And one could add a band to the 80s inheritors of that admirable mantle, Talk Talk.

When Talk Talk first hit the Top 20 in the autumn of 1982 with 'Today', they appeared very much in the mould of the moment. Sharing a label and a producer with Duran Duran, the band led by Mark Hollis also supported the Brummie pin-ups on tour in 1981, and the promo for 'Today' features all the 'Nice Video, Shame About the Song' clichés characteristic of the era. It seemed Talk Talk were merely the latest in an increasingly long line of poster-boys for the New Pop look and sound, ticking all the requisite boxes.

For those of us not paying attention when the band failed to deliver a string of big hit singles thereafter, it came as something of a surprise to see them re-emerge in startlingly different fashion during the drab uniformity of the immediate post-Live Aid period. Gone were the synth-pop trimmings and airbrushed cheekbones of 1982, replaced by something far more interesting. The first public outing of this change – at least in the band's homeland; other territories had been more receptive – was the 1986 single, 'Life's What You Make It', arguably one of the greatest hits of the entire decade and a track that manages the unique feat for a mid-80s recording in sounding just as fresh today as it did at the time.

'Life's What You Make It' was a trailer for the album 'The Colour of Spring', an organic soundscape at odds with the synthetic tapestry of mid-80s music and evidence that here was a band determined to do their own thing when corporate compromise was the order of the day. Critically acclaimed and (crucially) commercially successful, 'The Colour of Spring' gave Talk Talk the confidence to stretch their artistic wings even further. The result was 1988's 'Spirit of Eden', now rightly recognised as one of the decade's most significant and original masterpieces, yet its obstinate rejection of commercial considerations so panicked the band's label EMI at the time that it provoked a protracted court case as the band sought to escape their contract and any obligations to the record-buying masses.

Signing to Polydor's jazz offshoot Verve, Talk Talk then had to endure a familiar tactic from an ex-record label as EMI released a compilation album as soon as they'd gone; ironically, 1990's 'Natural History' went on to become the band's most successful LP in the UK, hitting the top three and prompting the re-release of 'It's My Life', which became Talk Talk's biggest British hit single. Whilst this belated celebration of the band's recent past was going on, Talk Talk were busy delving into more minimalist waters, resulting in the release of their final recording, 1991's 'Laughing Stock'. Refusal to return to the touring circuit or promote their output on television meant the album largely passed the public by, though the final two Talk Talk LPs are now hailed as important signposts en route to the so-called 'post-rock' of Radiohead and others. Despite this, the band – by the end reduced to an effective duo – split shortly after the release of 'Laughing Stock'; they remained true to their spirit by never succumbing to reunion-itis.

The band's leader and creative driving force Mark Hollis released an eponymous and solitary solo album in 1998, one that drew upon his passion for the sparse classical music and avant-garde jazz of the 50s and 60s, and then he largely withdrew from music altogether, citing the old MP reasons of 'spending time with his family' as he disappeared off the radar. Even when his influence was acknowledged by the next generation, such as his contribution to the 1998 Unkle album, 'Psyence Fiction', Hollis preferred to have his name removed from the credits. In an age in which overexposure is a virtue, Hollis's aversion to the spotlight seems incredibly refreshing, though the surprise announcement of his death at the age of 64 with only the 'after a short illness' explanation of his unfairly young demise seems characteristically obscure for a man who had long since come to the conclusion that the celebrity circus was not for him.

Now that the once all-powerful rule of the record companies has been laudably diminished by the rise of DIY bedroom recordings distributed by social media word-of-mouth, the likes of Mark Hollis and his aforementioned contemporaries and predecessors seem like prophets. Yes, the insidious corporate umbrella of UMG may well continue to churn out interchangeable and identikit fast-food marionettes for the kids, but the true artists survive on the periphery, as they always have and hopefully always will. Mark Hollis was one of them and his passing deserves to be marked.

Though trying to avoid every post being about the B word, the fact that most other news stories could compete with the B word in provoking despondency has pushed me back into familiar territory: the past. The odd detour through time is always a welcome break, and it's nice to take a detour for which directions were provided by an occasional commentator on here, 'Fred'. A 2017 post penned on the subject of the BBC's turn-of-the-80s gumshoe drama, 'Shoestring', saw said Fred recommend a precursor to Trevor Eve's private ear, 'Public Eye'.

Produced for the ITV network for an impressive ten years between 1965 and 1975, 'Public Eye' is quite a unique series from my own personal perspective in that even shows I didn't see a single episode of in the 1970s can be evoked via their theme tune or opening titles or even recollections of glimpsing trailers at the time. No such recollection exists for 'Public Eye'; I'd never heard of the programme until I was alerted to its existence and then I discovered it had quite a cult following amongst devotees of archive TV, particularly those on the restoration and preservation side such as the Kaleidoscope organisation. Recently, I found some episodes on YouTube and it only took a couple of viewings for me to realise it was very much up my street, so much so that a DVD box-set purchase was inevitable.

'Public Eye' stars Alfred Burke as enigmatic public inquiry agent, Frank Marker. Burke is an interesting-looking actor, resembling a cross between Will Self and ex-Leeds Utd boss Howard Wilkinson. Upon first viewing, he seemed to lack any strong personality for me in the part, but then I quickly realised that was the genius of the casting; a private eye needs to be anonymous, to blend in with the crowd and not stand out from it. A larger-than-life actor too handsome or charismatic would utterly defeat the object of the character and simply wouldn't convince. Marker's (and Burke's) strength is that he has an ordinariness about him that means nobody would notice if he was tailing them; they wouldn't spot him across the street, loitering in a shop doorway, pretending to make a call from a phone-box or supping a pint on the other side of the bar. He is perhaps television's most realistic and believable personification of a profession that has been a regular stand-by in TV drama for decades.

Frank Marker is a sharp operator, but not a shark; in comparison to the mercenary attitudes of fellow private detectives we meet during the course of the series, Marker is an honest man loath to fleece his clients. His honesty is rewarded with bouts of breadline living and – on one memorable occasion – a prison sentence for inadvertently being in possession of stolen goods. Prison hardens Marker even further, but Marker is a born lone wolf and a genuine man of mystery. His back-story is sometimes hinted at in dribs and drabs, but there is no big reveal; he doesn't appear to have many (if any) friends; he has few (if any) romantic interests – just imagine that in an equivalent series today; and he doesn't even employ a secretary. There is just him and his shabby raincoat, and a shabby succession of shabby offices.

ABC Television, one of the original ITV franchise holders, produced 'Public Eye' up until the company was succeeded by Thames in 1968; Thames then took over for the next seven years of the programme's run, overseeing the transition from monochrome to colour. But another factor that makes the series distinctive is the fact that Marker moves around. He begins his business in London, then relocates to Birmingham; after his spell behind bars, he moves on to Brighton, Windsor,

Walton, and finally ends up in Chertsey. The extensive location filming from the Birmingham period onwards provides viewers who even in the 60s were tired of the capital as the eternal backdrop a novel opportunity to enjoy adventures in unfamiliar surroundings.

'Public Eye' is not a period piece in the sense that many programmes of its era are. Surviving 60s episodes (an outrageous amount were wiped, as was the practice at the time) exhibit frequent and obvious references to homosexuality and not in a crude manner. One particularly effective episode guest-stars a young Stephanie Beacham as a troubled teen Marker saves from suicide. Her attempt at ending it all follows rejection by her presumed lover, 'Chris'. Marker's subsequent investigation uncovers the fact that Chris is in fact short for Christine rather than Christopher. The depressing world of vice rings is also covered with unexpected candour, and the pre-reform divorce laws provide regular cases back in the days when infidelity needed to be proven.

There are occasions when Frank Marker's often bristly antisocial attitude in regard to his closely-guarded independence is challenged. The Brighton episodes see him develop a potentially romantic relationship with his landlady and there are other interludes when he either works for a private inquiry agency or enters into a partnership. But none of these alliances last because he's a man made to be alone, both professionally and personally; some of us are just designed like that, and Frank Marker is a character that really gets under the skin – in the nicest possible way. There's a truth to him that's rare in television drama, when characters can easily slip into caricature as reality is overly-heightened. Soap operas profess to be rooted in realism, but exceeding reliance on ratings-grabbing stunts such as endless sieges, crashes, explosions, fires and murders has utterly diluted these claims in recent years.

'Public Eye' is not unlike the surviving 70s episodes of 'Dixon of Dock Green' in that its prime focus is on the little people and their relatable problems. The series largely steers clear of 'action' or melodrama. It's downbeat, sometimes melancholy, and there is sympathy for those who call upon Marker's services, most of whom are familiar faces to anyone who regularly binges on vintage TV that tends to get overlooked by the nostalgia industry. Many of its themes wouldn't be out-of-place in a contemporary drama, but the treatment these themes receive is a world away from today. An episode dealing with a deluded fantasist whose lies mask clinical depression is handled humanely and with an utter absence of sledgehammer moralising or facile 'U OK, hun?' *faux*-concern.

As a refreshing alternative to the here and now, cathode-ray windows to the past can sometimes remind one of what we've lost, what we've gained, and what we've retained. 'Public Eye' is a fine example of what British television used to do and could still do...if it wanted to.

BITTERSWEET SYMPHONIES
25 March 2019

Like Handel, Henry James and TS Eliot before him, Noel Scott Engel wasn't born in these islands but found what he was looking for here. He came all the way from Ohio expecting to arrive in an England populated by Ealing eccentrics like Margaret Rutherford; and by his own admission, the nation wasn't short of such characters once he touched down in Blighty. Scott Walker, an American-born British citizen since 1970, was one of ours. And now we've

119

lost him. Blessed with a mellifluous baritone voice that has influenced singers way beyond his own generation – everyone from David Bowie to Jarvis Cocker – Scott Walker went from being the definitive 60s pop balladeer to eventually exploring uncharted sonic waters in a series of challenging albums that acted as a foundation stone for the likes of Bjork, Radiohead and numerous others too many to mention. Yet for many, he remains the voice we return to whenever our hearts need healing. We'll get through it as long as Scott Walker is there for us.

They remain a small and select breed, and perhaps it's no surprise that genuine musical mavericks often spend the majority of their careers in the cult shadows, largely unrecognised by a wider public that can tell a Taylor Swift from an Ariana Grande. Scott Walker was relatively unusual in that he began his journey as a proper pop star. With John Maus and Gary Leeds, he headed a trio who adopted a shared surname and relocated to where the action was in 1965 – London.

It's perhaps easy to underestimate how exotically androgynous The Walker Brothers must have seemed in the mid-60s; even amidst the outré sartorial styles of Swinging London, they stood out; and from the distance of half-a-century, these unrelated male siblings still look strikingly cool in that uniquely effeminate male manner of the era. Unlike their contemporaries, the Walkers opted not for loud guitars, but instead salvaged the white pop ballad from the anodyne teen idols of the Brill Building production line, taking it onto an epic level of grandiosity that only Phil Spector could match at the time and laying the ground for The Bee Gees in the process. Good-looking guys coupled with sweeping symphonic standards even yer mum could whistle was a winning formula with teenyboppers alienated by the increasingly experimental edges of The Beatles, and for around eighteen months The Walker Brothers outsold all brands of sliced bread.

One of the last classic package tours of the 60s took place in early 1967, when the Walkers shared an unlikely bill with Cat Stevens, Engelbert Humperdinck...and Jimi Hendrix. Many cite this as the moment when the impending divide between pop and rock was sealed, yet it wasn't just Hendrix who realised he was playing before the wrong audience. For Scott Walker, the deafening din of screams drowning out every live performance (combined with frustration at having to interpret the songs of others when he was penning plenty of his own) prompted the inevitable split. He released his first solo LP in the autumn of '67, propelled high in the album charts courtesy of the sizeable fan following he could command; although still drenched in MOR trimmings, the presence of songs by Belgian chanson legend Jacques Brel pointed the way to a more ambitious sequence of albums ahead.

Scott Walker operated in a field of one on the UK music scene in the late 60s. On the surface, he was the antithesis of the prevailing culture, producing heavily-orchestrated pop immune to the period's musical innovations and he could even boast that emblem of unthreatening acceptance, his very own BBC TV show. However, Walker's easy-on-the-ear crooning was something of a canny Trojan horse as he sneaked far more subversive content under the noses of the light entertainment department. Yes, his galloping recital of Brel's 'Jackie' landed him in hot water with the new 'fun' Radio 1, but his albums continued to sell despite the risqué lyrical nature of his material; when his second solo LP topped the charts in 1968, it seemed as if his fan-base was prepared to follow Walker in whichever radical direction he was willing to take them.

Virtually alone in attempting to create a contemporary, baroque incarnation of the kind of dark, introspectively melancholy pop Frank Sinatra had pioneered a decade before with albums such as 'Only the Lonely', Scott Walker approached the 1970s confident he had manufactured and mastered an entirely new genre. Unfortunately, what many now regard as one of his finest works – 1969's 'Scott 4' – failed to chart; just as he was preparing to peak, his audience deserted him. It appeared the public only wanted a song stylist churning out Bacharach/David covers on mainstream TV variety shows after all. Perhaps reflecting his disappointment, the energy and inspiration went out of his work in the early 70s and it was only when The Walker Brothers reunited in 1975 – returning to the top ten with 'No Regrets' – that Scott seemed to get his mojo back.

The reunion ended with the 1978 album, 'Nite Flights', notable for the return of Scott as a songwriter as well as heralding the beginning of the more avant-garde, esoteric phase of his career that would define him for what remained of it. His cult credentials swelled in the early 80s, thanks to the Julian Cope-compiled album, 'Fire Escape in the Sky: The Godlike Genius of Scott Walker'; interest in this reclusive, enigmatic character was further rekindled with his first solo album in a decade, 1984's 'Climate of Hunter', but a further decade elapsed before his next effort, 1995's 'Tilt'. By now, Walker seemed to have found a niche (and a dedicated fan-base) for himself again, embracing minimalism and industrial sounds whilst delving into beguiling lyrical waters. He continued along this path and did so without a roadmap, releasing two more albums that became the benchmark for 'uneasy listening', 2006's 'The Drift' and 'Bish Bosch' (2012).

Whatever one's opinion of his later, critically-acclaimed efforts, one cannot but admire the curiosity of the artist in seeking to go where no man had gone before when the nostalgia circuit would have been the easy option; but remember, this a man who at the peak of his pop success in 1968 spent time in an Isle of Wight monastery studying Gregorian chant; Scott Walker rarely chose the easy option. And that's why he's worthy of all the imminent obituaries. Yes, the majority of these (like this) will focus on his time in the 60s spotlight, but there's little in his recorded output from that period to be ashamed of; even if some of the material could be called substandard filler, there's always that voice. Even when he was producing music so 'out there' that it made Stockhausen sound like The Archies, there was *always* that voice.

ABOUT A GIRL
5 April 2019

No other artistic medium can evoke past people and places with the speed and precision of music. Old songs are often intensely personal time capsules that, once unlocked years or even decades after they ceased to provide life with its soundtrack, can resurface as defining documents of who we were, where we were, and who were with when our ears last heard them. A few bars out-of-the-blue can put you back where you were in an instant, as though the moment is so deeply engrained in the grooves of the record that the moment is as intrinsic to the recording as the instrumentation; it can be impossible to separate the song from the moment.

For me, many works of favourite musicians and singers are so bound-up with the first time I was exposed to them that music and moment are genuinely inseparable; this is particularly potent if my affair with the artists in question was encapsulated in a brief burst of passion and I subsequently haven't kept in touch. Nirvana are a case in point, so associated with a precise period of my life that it's only because today marks 25 years since Kurt Cobain pointed a shotgun at his head that I've dug out 'Nevermind' and 'In Utero' and dusted them down (literally - the vinyl was filthy) to properly listen for the first time this century. The short 'n' sweet career of Nirvana – and the suicide of Kurt Cobain, which casts quite an ominous shadow over that career – makes me think of a friend of mine I haven't thought about for some time. For the purposes of this post, I shall call her Layla.

In 1994, Layla was my only friend in the neighbourhood, living a few doors away; she was seventeen and had just found out she was pregnant by a 'bad boy' that her parents (rightly, as it turned out) didn't approve of. Suddenly finding herself out of favour with the rather conservative mindset of that neighbourhood, I sensed she needed a friend who had long found that mindset as oppressive as she now did, and I was right. I'd known her for a few years as a neighbour, but we forged a close friendship as we began to spend more time in each other's company during what was a fairly traumatic year for her. A virtual pinball between boyfriend and family, she found refuge at my place as we stuck Nirvana on the turntable, chatted, consumed cup-after-cup of coffee, and chain-smoked for hours (yes, pregnant women still did in the early 90s).

Being a little older than Layla, it was refreshing to discover she was a Nirvana fan. Last time I'd asked her about music (when she was around 14), she'd been into New Kids on the Block. It reminded me how tastes change radically – and rapidly – in one's teens, but it meant I had the chance to provide her with some background, lending her LPs by The

Stooges, New York Dolls, Sex Pistols *et al*. I'd spent a while immersed in the Rave scene, finding guitar bands as irrelevant as Trad Jazz once the 90s dawned. Then there was that memorable performance of 'Smells Like Teen Spirit' on TOTP, when Kurt sang live and plummeted all the way down the scale to an Andrew Eldritch baritone-from-Hell as what had been safely secluded in the Indie ghetto abruptly gate-crashed the mainstream.

For a band stripped down to the (hard) core of a trio, Nirvana generated an immensely intense noise, but one punctuated by melodic passages that exposed pop sensibilities. Born the same year as me, Kurt Cobain shared my appetite for the pre-Punk rock that the 80s concept of 'cool' had told us we weren't allowed to like whilst the 80s simultaneously inflicted upon our ears the worst music imaginable, whether Bon Jovi or Rick Astley. Then those nice people at the music press did what they always did by coining a hideous name – 'Grunge' – to attach to Nirvana and the bands that charged through the doors Kurt and friends had inadvertently kicked down. Yes, the 'scene' (for what it was) quickly took on the shape of a bandwagon and burned out within a couple of years, but its most articulate practitioners at least gave us a welcome breather from what had gone immediately before.

I followed the soap opera of Kurt's marriage to Courtney Love of Hole in the music papers, but it was an amusing diversion from the good work being done – bringing the best rhetoric from the 'alternative' side of the tracks to a wider audience and in turn calling time on the embarrassingly antiquated attitudes and clichés of Guns 'n' Roses and their ilk. I doubted Axl Rose would have a clue who Sylvia Plath was, but I had a feeling Kurt Cobain knew. Yet, as with the late Mrs Hughes, there were numerous indications his time in the spotlight was destined to be short.

There was a kind of grim fatality to those lumbered with the 'Gen X' label, one that made the ending Kurt Cobain brought upon himself somehow inevitable. It radiated a resigned slacker surrender to the narrative that said everything important had been done in the 60s and 70s. 'Okay,' said Gen X, 'well I won't try then. I'll smoke dope, wear the same clothes for a week and grow my hair without bothering to wash it. And I'll listen to Black Sabbath as well as Black Flag.' What was adopted as the Grunge 'look' was merely a regional equivalent of my own adolescent anti-fashion, native to Seattle. Once 'Nevermind' established Nirvana as unlikely radio-friendly unit-shifters, it was of course co-opted by opportunistic designers, and the lumberjack shirt became as much of a dead-end uniform as Sid Vicious' leather jacket had been a few years before. Alas, nobody in 1994 foresaw Nirvana would one day join The Ramones in being reduced to a T-shirt.

Kurt Cobain's suicide – something heroin undoubtedly played a depressingly familiar part in – meant a great deal at the time because he was the first famous person of my generation to die. We'd grown up with all the legends of the so-called '27 Club', but they were historical figures to us – even if the death of the most recent (Jim Morrison) wasn't as far back in time then as Cobain's death is in 2019, scarily. News broke three days after the date of his demise; it was a Saturday. Radio 1's 'Evening Session' paid tribute a couple of days later; I still have an audiotape recording of it somewhere; I remember listening to it with Layla. We were subdued by the shocking passing of someone who mattered to us right at the moment when Layla herself was carrying a new life inside her. And the cycle goes on.

A few months after Kurt Cobain's messy exit, Layla gave birth to a little girl as Nirvana's morbidly beautiful

'Unplugged' LP was effortlessly sailing to the top of the charts. A few months after that, the cultural goalposts were shifted once again as Blur and Oasis prepared to lock horns; meanwhile, Layla was changing nappies, and I was getting ready to relocate elsewhere. Layla's mother thanked me for being a good friend to her daughter during the most difficult months; 'I don't know how she'd have managed without you,' she said, which was kind of her. I don't know how I'd have managed without Layla.

Years passed. Layla and I saw each other periodically as we both moved around with the restlessness of gypsies for a good decade, and then we did what so many once-close friends do – we lost touch. But whenever I recall Nirvana – which isn't, I admit, very often now – I recall Layla and a lovely friendship that grew out of alienation from our shared surroundings, one that had its perfect poet laureate in Kurt Cobain.

THE EYES OF A CHILD
15 April 2019

Aged three, I guess the saddest sentence in the English language for me was 'It's time for Andy Pandy to wave goodbye now'; it was infancy's equivalent of 'I've met someone else', though at least the end-of-the-world dejection was diluted by the promise of a return visit to Andy's place the following week: 'But he's coming again soon.' And he did, as did all of the inhabitants of television's toy-box, despite the fact I had no say over my rationed encounters with them. They were my friends before I had real friends, and I regularly indulge in pre-school reunions now that I'm no longer dependent on broadcasters to determine when I can see them again.

As much as I loved the characters when a member of the target demographic, I also loved the worlds they lived in – worlds that seemed familiar, but not quite. Mary, Mungo & Midge may have resided in a 60s tower block, but it was one of those 'moonbase' 60s tower blocks as they looked on the architect's drawing-board before being built – sleek, space-age, analogue erections surrounded by green and pleasant land, as though these buildings had sprouted from the soil like beautiful, synthetic mushrooms; it was a modernist marriage of architecture and nature that never happened, a future that failed to arrive.

The wider townscape of this tower block's location was a similarly simplistic palette of pulsating primary colours, presenting an idyllic urban environment on a par with those illustrated in the Ladybird books of the era. If a child had designed this imaginary garden city, I wouldn't have been surprised; ditto Festive Road, address of Mr Benn, or Trumpton. When young children portray their surroundings in the galleries that decorate classrooms, their impressions generally stick to an endearingly primitive template that bears little resemblance to the actual surroundings their parents would recognise as home. Yet, chances are these parents would have depicted the world in an identical fashion when the same age, the age in which the visual is still the senior partner to the verbal where self-expression is concerned. At what point do we cease to see the world through our original eyes? And why, by the time we are in a position to shape that world, are the end results are so bloody ugly?

It was exquisite timing that the shows my generation watched with mother were all produced at the back-end of the 60s and beginning of the 70s; the creations of Oliver Postgate, Gordon Murray, John Ryan and David McKee belonged to a brief moment of English pop culture in which a child's vision of the world was transplanted from the infant interior to the adult exterior. Amazing footage of the Technicolor boutiques lining the King's Road from this period bear it out; the lysergic Alice in Wonderland vibe of the shops spills out of the child's enchanting imagination and onto a grownup monochrome pavement in a way that gleefully contradicts the accepted narrative of maturity; the wares on display also have a childlike charm that adults usually lose and rarely recover.

There's a distinct difference between childlike and child*ish*, however. The former is the retention of an optimistic, prepubescent perspective on aesthetics that can sit comfortably alongside more advanced attitudes to topics the prepubescent mind struggles with. By contrast, the latter is a thumb-sucking rejection of the childlike, a voluntary regression into the facsimile womb of so-called 'kidulthood', a onesie-clad Neverland that refuses to progress beyond the safe space of its own emotionally-retarded playground and responds to any incursion of the adult world with tears and tantrums. Childlike can be compatible with 'grownup'; childish is wilfully negative and has little connection with the genuine child that is always desperate to be older than it actually is; the genuine child is forever looking forward to a world it has already designed in an imagination bursting with brilliantly bonkers ideas, inventing an exciting adult landscape that is uniquely childlike in its conception.

I have friends whose homes are an Aladdin's Cave of delightful kitsch and individual eccentricities, decorated with broken old toys and other ornaments with the sole function of raising a smile. But these friends are not intellectual imbeciles; they have merely achieved an admirable equilibrium between child and adult that blends the best of both worlds to form a better one. When governments award multimillion-pound contracts to private companies to take charge of our environment and its institutions, the only beneficiaries are those involved in the transaction. I know if my aforementioned friends were awarded such a contract, we'd all benefit; they'd not only do it for free but they'd transform neighbourhoods so they resembled Pepperland before the Blue Meanies got their hands on it. Most five-year-olds would do the same; their 35-year-old selves, on the other hand, designed what we're lumbered with.

A childlike side can be a potent aesthetic weapon worth utilising and I only wish more of those who design and construct our surroundings did. Perhaps then the look of our schools, workplaces, homes, hospitals and streets wouldn't instil such depression whenever we have cause to be there. Our environment acts as a mirror; we see grey, we feel grey; we see ugly, we feel ugly – ulcers begat ulcers. There's not much knife-crime in Chipping Norton, I'll wager. Lest we forget, Oscar Wilde's response when asked in the US why American society was prone to violence was 'Because your wallpaper is so terrible'. Think about it.

The system drills the childlike out of most children and the adult that emerges as a fully-processed sausage at the end of the conveyor belt has been remade and remodelled to live by an approved script of league tables, life insurance, pension schemes, profit margins, mortgages, and an absolute absence of imagination. He has nostalgic moments of wistful remembrance, recalling his five-year-old self; but his education has taught him he cannot connect with that child and he consequently believes him to be irretrievable. He isn't, though it depends how far one has been absorbed into the system or how much one has become one's mother or father without putting up a fight.

Trying not to entirely lose the view of the world when seen through the wide eyes of a child isn't easy and it is true that some circumstances are more conducive to it than others. Similarly, there is always the temptation to cling to the childlike simply as a refuge to flee into the comforting embrace of whenever headlines overwhelm and enrage. But it can be salvaged; it needs to be. I've resisted evoking the Jesuit motto, *'Give me a child until he is seven and I will give you the man'*, but it's a saying that retains its relevance if turned round: *'Give me the man and I will give you a child of seven'.* He's still there in all of us, and he still has a lot to offer. Don't ignore him. I am he as you are he as you are me - and we are all together.

ABSENT FRIENDS
7 May 2019

One of the many highlights on the landmark 1968 Kinks album, 'The Village Green Preservation Society' is a song called 'Do You Remember Walter?' The narrator fondly recalls a childhood sidekick in a series of anecdotal reminiscences that celebrate Walter's semi-heroic status – 'Do you remember Walter playing cricket in the thunder and the rain?/Do you remember Walter smoking cigarettes behind your garden gate?' Gradually, the tone of the lyrics alters as the narrator acknowledges his wistful curiosity over what became of his old mate will no doubt be dampened by the inevitable and humbling reality of time passing – 'I bet you're fat and married/and you're always home in bed by half-past eight'. The singer of the song concludes with detectable melancholy, 'Walter, you are just an echo of a world I knew so long ago/Walter, if you saw me now, you wouldn't even know my name.' The song speaks volumes because we all have a Walter and we've all wondered 'Whatever happened to..?'

Take Joey. Joey was my first 'best mate' when I started school, the first kid who joined me in a playground re-enactment of a 'Top of the Pops' performance from the night before ('Blockbuster' by The Sweet, in case you were wondering); barely six months after I started school, however, my parents relocated us all to another part of town and the friendship ceased to exist overnight. The last time I saw Joey was the summer of 1973, and that's where he remains in my head. As children have a slim grasp of a past too brief to linger in, their permanent presence in the present means they can shrug off the loss of one friendship and quickly move on to the next without dwelling on it; I did just that several times over the next couple of years, when my family imposed nomadic social mobility on my education. I thus became accustomed to the idea of friendship as a short-term arrangement; but as the casualties began piling up, I eventually started to wonder where those fading faces had faded to.

What just one standout vignette in an entire LP of them says about absent friends is both touching and potent – how the flesh-and-blood of the here and now invariably dissolves into the ether of memory as tomorrow supersedes today. People it can be impossible to imagine our lives without will all vacate the present tense and find their way to the cemetery of friendship in the end; and the longer we live, the more crowded that cemetery becomes. When a resident of it gatecrashes our thoughts without warning - an unexpected intrusion often triggered by stumbling upon something they were associated with - we pause, attempting to picture their face. We try to reconstruct that countenance as it might have aged when we were no longer looking at it; it's a mental equivalent of those strange imagined impressions of the adult that a missing child could have morphed into, ones the police produce to complete cold cases. We can't quite do it, though, for lost friends are indeed the living dead, frozen phantoms preserved in our internal graveyard that never grow old.

Yes, it is true that we can disentangle ourselves from family if we so wish, though the intricate web of emotional blackmail many families survive by can make such a move a minefield; with friends, it's different. Friends were *our* choice, those we instinctively gravitated towards because there was a connection we discerned that meant more than a mere shared surname. As the old saying goes, you can judge a man by the company he keeps – and the choice of our friends is an expression of us as individuals. This is especially important when we are children.

As a child kicks and pushes its way out of the infant egg, part of the hatching process is establishing a life beyond the confines of mum and dad; forming friendships is a crucial aspect of that process, enabling the child to make its first independent mark in the world free from the parental CCTV. We therefore naturally develop a possessive bond with our chosen companions that can sometimes manifest itself as loyalty blinding us to faults and failings we prefer to believe are the exclusive province of those we didn't pick for our private football team, i.e. family. What, indeed, does it say about us or our judgement should our cherished friends be exposed as owning feet composed of clay? When they betray or abandon us, it hurts because we expected better from them; we anticipate being let down by family, but not by friends. Forgiving is hard enough; forgetting can be even harder.

Social media can put people back in touch, this is true; but is that such a wise endeavour? I know one friend who has done just that more than once and the outcomes have not always been happy; sometimes it's best to leave well alone and keep the recollection intact and unsullied by the passage of time.

Charles Dickens carried a torch for adolescent sweetheart Maria Beadnell, his first love; but the torch was abruptly snuffed out after years of burning bright in his heart when he met up with her in middle age, long after she had roused his nascent passions; he imagined she would still be as he remembered her. She wasn't. Indeed, any form of high school reunion can be fraught with dangers that stretch back decades. We never forget the friends who let us down, but do we recall the ones *we* let down? Who knows what bitter resentments we may have inadvertently fostered in the memories of others? We may be disappointed to see our own Walter 'fat and married', but what of those to whom *we* are Walter? Memory has the capacity to be a uniquely selective tonic.

Each act of my existence has come with its own repertory company of players, and very few have remained with the company for long. There is rarely any crossover between productions either; there tends to be a fresh crop of actors for every new script. Such a scenario often imbues the leader of the company with a rootless insecurity and a feeling of belonging nowhere; this is a direct outcome of those blink-and-you'll-miss-'em blood brothers of childhood. There are times when I envy those who have stayed in touch with most of the friends they've made in their lives; there are other times when I wonder if such a network can be as much of an impediment to personal progress as family can be. Granted, some friends had a sole role, that of facilitating the next phase; once the next phase was here, they had gone; others should have stuck around a little longer. Some I don't miss and have no desire to reunite with whatsoever; others were worthy of eternity and their disappearance left behind a black hole that still radiates the sense of something missing, something that would have continued to enrich my life had it remained.

One of the trickier elements of this constant changing of characters is that there can be gaps between an outgoing cast and an incoming one – and these gaps have a habit of gradually widening on each occasion they come around. At the moment, I'm reduced to monologues; I recently staged a one-man show that spanned seven days, playing to an empty theatre every night. But, hell, I've been here before and I've always managed to recruit an audience eventually. I ain't panicking. I guess at times it can be hard not to envy the child's lack of a past and stoic ability to forge ahead free from being haunted by the lost; the only thing a child can glimpse when he looks back over his shoulder is a void - and it's far better to have the void behind than in front, for sure.

So, yes, to answer the question posed by Ray Davies fifty years ago, I *do* remember Walter - lots of Walters. But where are they now, those collective Walters that contributed so much to the weaving of this tatty tapestry now looking distinctly frayed at the edges? No idea, but thanks for the memories, wherever you are – hopefully healthy, wealthy and wise, passing through the lives of others like you passed through mine.

ABOUT BRITAIN
17 May 2019

'Community', like many words, has changed its meaning somewhat over the last few decades. At one time, community used to be a geographical term, one generally applied to describe the mixed residents of a neighbourhood, town, city or county. By contrast, today it seems every niche interest or lifestyle can lay claim to the word, and everyone who subscribes to an approved social demographic has its own community on the 21st century bus-route. Over-familiar phrases such as 'The LGBT Community' or 'The Muslim

135

Community' to some appear a tad patronising, assuming anyone who happens to fall into one of these categories is somehow the member of an exclusive tribe; and each tribe appears to regard mere membership itself as the defining characteristic of its members. The proliferation of self-contained groups that refer to themselves as communities may give comfort to those who seek like-minds, but it often feels like the definition of the word has been narrowed in the process.

Forty-five years ago, when community still retained its earlier, far broader meaning, the prevalent distinctions between different parts of the country were perceived to be at risk from the threat of nationwide homogenisation; the Wilson Government had already ring-fenced the Welsh language at a time when it was verging on extinction, and moves were afoot to consciously reinforce regional identity throughout the UK via a revived medium. With the challenge of the pirates still fresh in the ears of listeners, the broadcasting stranglehold of the BBC was belatedly broken in government-sanctioned fashion by the arrival of Independent Local Radio. This was commercial television's audio offshoot, one that transformed the ITA into the IBA and began to spread like a wireless virus across the country following the 1973 debut of LBC and Capital Radio in London.

BBC local radio had arrived in the aftermath of the network station reorganisation in 1967, but had largely been a rather conservative enterprise, appealing mainly to pensioners and followers of local football teams. Here was a more dynamic, perhaps more American notion of a radio station, however – built around a top 40 playlist peppered with programmes designed with the locality in mind and ads unique to the area covered by the transmitter. As with the individual ITV franchise holders of the era, loyalty to the region in question was fostered with these ILR stations; indeed, it was partly their *raison d'être*. Their very names reflected the regions they broadcasted to, usually named after a geographical feature, such as a river – Radio Clyde (Glasgow), Radio Orwell (Ipswich), Radio Trent (Nottingham), Radio Tees (Stockton), and Radio Aire (Leeds) being notable examples.

There was a deliberate effort on the part of these new additions to the local landscape to represent the areas they transmitted to with pride, appealing to the community spirit in listeners to keep them from turning to the national BBC stations. At times, the aping of the Radio 1 style with a regional twist could be hopelessly naff; promotional material featuring DJs looking like Tony Blackburn tribute acts were abundant in the pages of the IBA's annual 'Television and Radio' guidebook, and the mid-Atlantic accent often sat uncomfortably alongside regional dialect on the airwaves – a factor that was fictionalised with shrewd accuracy in the shape of Bristol-based Radio West on BBC TV's 'Shoestring'. But the ILR operation nonetheless gave every impression of being a success by the sheer number of stations that began to appear.

Between 1974 and 1976, no less than sixteen ILR stations opened; there was then a four-year sabbatical before further expansion from 1980 onwards. Over the next seven years, a staggering 38 more ILR stations were added to the roll-call, so that by the end of the 80s, virtually every old-school 'community' was commercially catered for. And then it all came to a shuddering halt with Margaret Thatcher's final fixing of an unbroken system before the Poll Tax called time on the Thatcherite project, the 1990 Broadcasting Act.

In television terms, the Broadcasting Act enabled the BBC to fall into the fatal hands of John Birt and for ITV to self-destruct into the corporate car-crash that eventually brought us Cowell and Kyle. With radio, the damage was arguably even more profound and was further exacerbated by the deregulation of the Communications Act 13 years later. The dissolution of the IBA and the establishment of a new regulatory body with a remit to issue new licences to the highest bidder were reflective of a different approach to commercial radio. A series of mergers and buyouts and the replacement of specialised regional broadcasting with networked generic programming after-dark altered the ILR template so their stations became less a hallmark of regional identity and more an amateurish alternative to slick new national stations such as Virgin, without being especially distinguishable from them. Indeed, what was the point in tuning-in to the poor relation country-cousin if there was no distinction between a local station and a national one?

The old definition of community was dispensed with as the 20th century drew to a close; it was no longer about where you are, but *what* you are. The sudden rash of new stations saw a cluttered diversification that effectively created radio ghettos in which community was redesigned along genre lines when it came to the playlist; the fictitious oldies stations often heard playing in the background of Peter Kay's comedy series such as 'Car Share' are uncannily accurate parodies of how unlistenable the real thing can be. Another example was coverage of, and commentary on, local football teams – always a big draw for the ILR stations; in many cases, copyright transferred to the clubs themselves (especially if they dined at the Premier League table); this symbolic shaving-off of key elements of the old-school ILR station has continued so that every community today has its radio voice and preaches solely to the converted.

Now splintered into hundreds of little communities, the fragmented airwaves undoubtedly possess a greater range of that arch-Thatcherite word, 'choice', than ever before. But the original aim behind the formation of Independent Local Radio is essentially as dead a concept as the past contrasts between different parts of the country, and Independent Local Radio as a label itself is a complete misnomer today. Have we lost something? Perhaps community as a broader term and this then being mirrored by broadcasters has been a notable casualty. The differences between us have always been abundant, but during the ILR's heyday, these differences seemed to unite us under one genuinely 'diverse' umbrella. The differences now are so myriad that they seem more prone to division – and in some cases, voluntary segregation. But at least, to paraphrase Peter Kay's Chorley FM, there's always a radio station 'coming in your ear'.

BLING AND A PRAYER
19 May 2019

No wonder no one knows where we stand with Europe. Two European club competitions and the finals of both are being contested between English teams – Liverpool Vs Spurs in the Champions League (formerly known as the European Cup) and Arsenal Vs Chelsea in the Europa League (formerly known as the UEFA Cup), the first time four teams from the same nation have filled the two European finals of what those nice people at the BBC and the Grauniad insist we refer to as 'the *men's* game'; and yet none of the four teams in question are our peerless domestic treble victors, Manchester City. On the same day City thrashed Watford 6-0 – registering the largest winning margin in an FA Cup Final for over a century – the man flying the flag for the UK on the Continent crashed and burned all the way to the bottom of the heap in Tel Aviv.

139

Earlier in the day (maybe as a means of subconscious preparation), I watched the 1974 Eurovision Song Contest in full on YouTube – yes, and I have indeed lived to tell the tale. Held at the Brighton Dome, 1974 was the year four Swedes famously captured the crown; but over-exposure to Abba's win with 'Waterloo' had made me ignorant of other entries that would perhaps have won in any other year, such as the exquisite 'Si' by Italy's Gigliola Cinquetti, up there with 'L'amour est bleu' by Vicky Leandros in 1967 as arguably the best Eurovision song never to have won the Eurovision.

1974 was a time when the Eurovision was still an MOR showbiz showcase for all the family, held in theatres in which evening dress appeared to be compulsory, and presented by a middle-aged lady looking like a Home Counties hostess at a W.I. Tory Party fundraiser. But the tournament was very much in transitional mode 45 years ago – trapped between the post-'Puppet on a String' oompah formula whilst simultaneously trying to capture the Glam Rock spirit of the moment, falling into a strange limbo with one foot in both camps yet being at home in neither. Despite this uneasy mix, the 1974 contest when viewed in its entirety remains a relentlessly entertaining way to spend a couple of hours.

At some point in the 90s, the Eurovision finally surrendered its last lingering pretensions to be taken seriously, with the rather stiff commentary of David Vine in 1974 superseded by the increasingly arch observations of Terry Wogan. But in losing its terminally unfashionable image, it was gradually reinvented as a camp, kitsch (and rather gay) carnival. The 1998 transgender triumph of Israel's Dana International, paving the way for the 2014 win of Austria's 'bearded lady' Conchita Wurst, was a landmark example of the event's repositioning as a celebration of pan-European 'diversity'. Those whose previous platform could have been the likes of the Alternative Miss World drag-fest or Channel 4's late-night 90s cult hit, 'Euro Trash', now had a near-global outlet in which a style of outré entertainment that had always inhabited the fringes could be belatedly normalised.

Regardless of the contest's eternal irrelevance in the USA, the huge viewing figures it can command across Europe (and, lest we forget, Australasia) were tempting enough to persuade long-time Dorothy acquaintance Madonna to take part as an interval act last night. Having lost touch with the career of an artist I once kept tabs on for decades, I watched Madonna's somewhat shaky performance of 'Like A Prayer' with interest, and despite the dodgy 'Sunday Night at the Palladium' effect of a once-important act reduced to reliving past glories at a glitzy variety show, Madonna actually appeared to have found her natural (rest) home, like Elvis settling in Vegas when the 60s were at their revolutionary height.

The voting section of the programme used to be my favourite part, but the sheer volume of participating nations today has cut short requests for the results of the respective juries; the show seemed to quickly zoom through presenter banter with satellite-linked announcers standing in front of a superimposed capital city backdrop and headed straight onto the outcome of 'The People's Vote'. This new innovation saw the pattern of the 'professional' juries turned upside down as the viewer's voting significantly altered the scoreboard when it was added to those votes already counted at the climax of the programme. North Macedonia had built up a good lead that was then completely overturned while the UK's representative, Michael Rice, stopped hovering hopefully above the relegation zone and sank to rock bottom. At least Lynsey de Paul and Mike Moran finished runners-up with an entry of that name in 1977 rather than 26th out of 26.

One would imagine Europe had learnt not to sanction any form of 'people's vote', as such gifts bestowed by rulers upon ruled have a habit of deviating from the script; but the outcome of Eurovision 2019 was very much decided by 'The People' – and they chose the Netherlands for the first time since 1975. Bar the traditional Greece/Cyprus love-in, there didn't appear to be much of the political bias that has marred the voting procedure in recent years; even Russia received a cheer this time round, but it paid to remember the precise location of this year's Contest and the contentious issues outside of the Eurovision bubble. Perhaps everyone was more than a little sensitive to these issues to resist using the event for making a point – with the exception of Iceland's bizarre entry flashing a few Palestinian scarves in the green-room.

Another interesting difference between the Eurovision of 45 years ago and today was the way in which every measly point tossed in the direction of the UK last night was received with somewhat pathetic gratitude. The British entry in 1974 – Olivia Newton-John – finished fourth with the dismally plodding 'Long Live Love', yet this result was no doubt greeted at the time as a national humiliation for a country accustomed to at least managing second place (as we have on fifteen separate occasions). In 2019, the 'plucky Brit' bollocks that has its roots in Eddie the Eagle means we settle for finishing in last place with a shrug of the shoulders; we expected no better even before the latest 'X-Factor' leftover delivered his forgettable ditty like a shy child hoping for relieved parental applause when overcoming nerves to mumble his one line at the school nativity play.

So, we are simultaneously the masters of Europe (in football) and its laughing stock (in pop). There's a point to be made somewhere in there when it comes to this country's attitude towards the Continent and Europe's attitude towards us, but I fear it could be lost in translation; perhaps Massiel, the Spanish entry of 1968 – whose controversial win over Cliff's 'Congratulations' was allegedly aided by General Franco – got it right when she kept it simple. *La, la, la...*

THE STORY OF US
7 June 2019

The wry, dry detachment of Larkin's oft-quoted observation on the cultural significance of 1963 – 'which was rather late for me' – makes me wonder if the old monochrome Britain still languishing in the shadow of war vanished forever when the last clump of snow from the unprecedented winter that opened this most transformative of years belatedly melted away in March. As the thaw began, The Beatles hit No.1 for the first time and pointed towards a new kind of Britain. Britain was ready for it. The Profumo Scandal exposed the decadent double-standards of the ruling elite, whereas deference received a further kicking when Ronnie Biggs and his mob robbed Her Majesty's mail train. To borrow the catchphrase of Danny Boon, the cheesy comedian from 'Billy Liar' (released in 1963), 'It's all happening!' And it was.

The pieces were already in place – from the satire boom to the 'kitchen sink' school of cinema and theatre – and were evident on the country's newest and most influential medium, television. The spread of the ITV network across the UK was complete by 1963 and the ITV company that had broken the mould of drama with 'Coronation Street', Granada, also revitalised current affairs broadcasting with 'World in Action', whose brash, fearless, innovative attitude contrasted dramatically with the somewhat staid 'Panorama' and its avuncular host, Richard Dimbleby. It's doubtful whether the BBC would have commissioned a study of the British class system as seen through the eyes of specially-selected seven-year-olds; but 'World in Action' did. The timing, like so much that happened here in 1963, was right.

Watching the original 'Seven Up' documentary now, it's clear the year was on a cusp and not quite 'Swinging'; indeed, it's remarkable how Edwardian it all looks when showing the children in the school environment. The working-class kids are crammed into those austere red-brick fortresses most of us attended, whereas the public school lot remain locked in a 'Tom Brown' bubble, reciting 'Waltzing Matilda' in Latin and enduring military drills overseen by a fascistic little prefect. The characteristic bigging-up to impress peer groups is blatant at both ends of the social scale – the posh boys declaring they read the Financial Times and the tenement scamp claiming he goes to bed at either 10 or 11 o'clock. These children may not have been media-savvy, but they are remarkably self-assured.

As a one-off, 'Seven Up' stands on its own as a unique document of a country caught on camera just before the start of the social transformations that the children of 1963 would gradually benefit from. We may well have been left to guess what awaited them, but then something special happened. When a young researcher on 'Seven Up' called Michael Apted was asked to direct a follow-up programme seven years later, he tracked down the 14 participants, and the comparisons between the charismatic kids of 'Seven Up' and the moody, awkward adolescents of '7 Plus Seven' was a fascinating snapshot of lives in transition. Apted says at that moment he realised the potential of what he had on his hands.

The greatest contrasts between then and now take place in the first three instalments of what became an ongoing series, and the contrasts aren't merely physical or in the hairstyles and fashions. In 1977, Apted reunited the 14 again for '21 Up', when the young adults were reaping the rewards of the decade that began with the first programme. Although the five participants to go through the private and public school systems – Charles, Andrew, John, Bruce and Suzy – had all travelled the educational routes already mapped-out for them in 'Seven Up', others denied their privileges were making their way in a way that reflected the social mobility revolution: farmer's son Nick and suburban Scouser Peter were both at university, whereas the three East End girls – Jackie, Lynn and Sue – were all earning enough to buy their own homes; this factor makes '21 Up' seem as distant now as the original documentary. However, perhaps the first real indication that some of these lives were destined to make a massive emotional impact on the audience came with Neil in '21 Up'.

The bright and bubbly buddy of Peter in 'Seven Up' had dropped-out of university after failing to fulfil the academic expectations of his parents and was doing menial work whilst living in a London squat. His frustration and sense of failure seem to convey world-weariness beyond his years; for the viewers, Neil's story touched a real nerve and became the most gripping of all. Seven years later, there was genuine shock when he appeared in '28 Up', hitchhiking his way through the Scottish highlands and of no fixed abode. Displaying nervous tics, clad in ill-fitting charity shop clothes and his hair shorn, he confessed 'I can't see any immediate future at all'. He looked dangerously like a man who had run out of everything.

Neil didn't fit the era's image of an economic casualty as seen in, say, 'Boys from the Blackstuff' (i.e. a victim of deindustrialisation); he was more an early casualty of the collapse of social mobility's aspirations, someone who had fallen through the cracks from the lower middle-classes. His struggles have formed the series' most compelling narrative; every time it comes around, Neil's update is always left till last. There was a touching intervention at one stage from fellow participant Bruce, demonstrating the compassion that had been visible in his seven-year-old ambition to become a missionary (one member of the family who seems to have fulfilled the Jesuit maxim at the heart of the show's remit). Bruce offered Neil the spare bedroom and formed a friendship that enabled Neil to get back on his feet. Being a Lib Dem councillor and a lay-preacher seemed to give Neil a degree of purpose he'd so painfully lacked in earlier instalments, but his troubled past means viewers always fear the worst every seven years whilst simultaneously hoping for the best.

Our concern for Neil is potent because this remarkable project has provoked an emotional investment in its participants that means we genuinely care what happens to them. We see the stages of life unfold through them; as they age, their parents die but their offspring provide them with grandchildren. We see their hair going grey and sometimes fade away; we see their waistlines expand; but we also see them achieve something approaching contentment. Most have even managed a level of resigned acceptance with the intrusion of the series into their lives, something that has sometimes been manifested as bristly resentment resulting in the odd absence from an instalment.

But, of course, the older they get, the closer creeps their mortality. Cockney cabbie Tony has suffered health scares, farmer's son and physicist Nick is seriously ill with cancer, and – saddest of all – librarian Lynn passed away just a year after '56 Up', the first of the gang to die. Yet, this is life; there is tragedy, but there is triumph. Barnardo's boys Paul and Symon are two of the most grounded participants of all – both having a tough start in life yet reaching near-retirement age comfortable in their own skins. And this ninth instalment of a programme that stands as a towering tribute to the human spirit ended with a wonderfully elegiac shot of Neil riding his bike, musing on the collapse of his marriage. 'The idea of true love, which I think exists, occurs so seldom,' he says. 'If it occurs once in somebody's life, they're extremely lucky; for it then to happen, and then the potential can't be fulfilled, is heartbreaking.'

Always moving, but never sentimental – the 'Up' series really is an unparalleled example of what television as a medium is capable of and so rarely aims for. It was a product of its time, *our* time. We won't see its like again.

TRANSFORMER
7 August 2019

Adolescence may well be a transitional phase for both body and mind, but there's also a uniquely sartorial chameleon element to this odd interlude between childhood and adulthood that is crucial to finding who you are; it's as though you need to sample a series of brands on the shelves of the cultural supermarket before you eventually find the one that fits, the one you'll most probably stick with for the rest of your life (most usually pick their favourite at some point of their 20s). Of course, some remain admirably restless and resist 'settling down' with the same pair of trousers, whereas others – from the geriatric biker to the retired stockbroker – located their comfort zone forty or fifty years ago and have stayed there.

As a teenager, the swift shift from one social group to another – gravitating towards those with shared interests and passions – is marked by the taking-on of each new clique's appearance with unconscious ease. It's very much a natural adolescent habit for teenagers to instinctively tailor their look to match the crowd they're with; and for all the adolescent claims of 'individuality', the pack mentality inculcated in the playground creates a craving for like-minds and the desire for a tribe to belong to outside of the school gates. It also helps if the new hair colour or item of clothing that earns membership of said crowd meets with parental disapproval; all part of the necessary severance of the apron strings, even if the economic climate of this particular century means the ever-changing wardrobe is usually funded by the Bank of Mum & Dad.

Looking back, I think I wore around half-a-dozen completely contrasting hairstyles (of various lengths and colour) between the ages of 13 and 23, all of them usually prompted by falling in love with a band or youth subculture; unfortunately, my own personal experience was of a constant failure to find anyone else who shared a love of whatever prompted the annual visual regeneration, but most are lucky and locate a 'set'. Even so, I do recall certain acquaintances I had in the 80s who I'd bump into maybe once or twice a year, and every time I saw them they'd changed radically from our previous encounter just a few months before. That doesn't really happen at any other time of life.

It goes without saying that the longer you live, the lengthier can become the gaps between bumping into acquaintances; and if there *has* been a radical change in their appearance when your paths cross again, it's usually not one they've chosen (unlike during adolescence). Once you reach your 40s – or 50s – the main differences you notice when reuniting with people you knew 20 or 30 years before are the wrinkles, the waistline and the grey hairs (if there's any hair left). Perhaps one reason why some recall their teenage years with fondness is that it was the one time of their lives when they felt in control of their destinies, a time when they had yet to succumb to hopeless defeatism via the demands of the workplace, they hadn't been worn-out and wearied by children, and they remained a long way from being at the mercy of the aches and pains that accumulate with the passing decades.

Nonetheless, such chameleon traits are not the exclusive province of adolescents. Some continue to utilise this ability to blend into their constantly changing surroundings when it comes to relationships, so that each new partner has a different version of the same person that their predecessor had. Sensing the kind of man, woman or non-binary individual one's latest other half is subconsciously searching for can result in a subtle alteration from what the previous partner required. We often notice it in the recently-divorced when arm-in-arm with their post-'decree absolute' lover, looking distinctly different from the way they dressed when alongside their ex. A change of image can therefore result in both partners visually complementing one another for the duration of their relationship, settling into items of clothing they'd never before worn or expressed a preference for. Not necessarily 'they look just like two gurus in drag', but John & Yoko understood – as indeed did the first wife in the Lennon marital bed; Cynthia admitted adopting a 'peroxide Parisian' look in the early days of her relationship with John mainly because she was aware of his lustful yearnings for Brigitte Bardot.

This strange way in which lovers or spouses can suppress their own identities in order to keep their other half happy was brought home to me when I was researching my book about a dear departed friend name of Alison (veteran readers may recall the story). Her son told me of a point in the 1990s when she'd hooked-up with a bit of a flash twat who lived somewhere in the Little Venice neighbourhood of London; he noticed his mother seemed to be adopting this guy's taste for material goods in a way that had never been a hallmark of her personality before. He recalled her sudden interest in 'designer gear' with both bemusement and amusement, for it appeared so out of character with the woman he knew.

Alison's experience makes me aware that - if they're not careful - some risk being solely defined by their other half, as if they were unwittingly conditioned into sacrificing personal development in favour of constant companionship from too young an age, forever refashioning themselves to suit whoever they happened to be with. Should their voluntary role as an appendage come to an end, perhaps the fear of trying to survive without that clear definition – and being suddenly confronted by the unnerving absence of a personal identity outside of a relationship – propels them straight into ill-advised dalliances with unsuitable successors. Alison was a parent too, another factor by which women in particular can be exclusively defined in denial of who they might actually be. The Alison I knew seemed to be very much her own person, but she *had* lived alone for a number of years by this stage, so that might have helped her become the unique and original individual I remember. Anyway, I digress once again.

As I was saying, the cliché of time moving at a slower speed when younger could probably account for the breathless pace of the constant changes of image and tastes that can characterise adolescence; so much is crammed into a relatively short space that the memory tends to recall months as years and years as decades. I know from my own experience how the period from around 1983 up to roundabout 1993 (which retrospectively feels like a quarter-of-a-century) saw so many alterations in appearance that it's just as well I never had a passport. Chances are I'd have confused more than one customs official when switching his gaze from photo to person.

At about 40, I felt as if I'd found the character I'd been putting together for 25 years, albeit one who remains a work-in-progress; there's always room for improvement, though I have my sartorial side sorted now. If Fenella Fielding had managed to persuade Peter Wyngarde to have a crack at batting for the other side just for one night of passion, I'd probably have been the product of that fantastically *louche* liaison. Who says dreams die when you turn 21?

HIRSUTE YOU, SIR!
9 August 2019

Every politician who ascends to the ultimate seat of power seeks to impose their own values and ideas upon the premiership, and though all talk the talk when taking office, few actually have the genuine vision and skill to make real their radical proposals. Peter the Great, Tsar of Russia from 1682-1725, was one of the legendary historical rulers whose ambition was largely realised, especially the cultural revolution he recognised as necessary if his vast lumbering empire was to be dragged out of the middle ages. Influenced by his tour of Western Europe and exposure to Enlightenment thinking, he returned home determined to instigate change. But along with all the political, social and scientific overhauls, there were more instantly noticeable aesthetic alterations; he had taken note of European style, particularly how all the leading figures he was introduced to were clean-shaven.

Imposing heavy taxes on the wearers of beards in Peter the Great's Russia is perhaps one of the more seemingly trivial changes introduced by this reforming Romanov; but he saw the removal of hardcore facial hair – a long-standing tradition

151

in Russia – as key to his country moving closer to the great nations of Europe by presenting its ruling class as indistinguishable from the French, Austrian or English. A century later, the Prussian hero of Waterloo, General von Blücher, caused a stir during the celebrations in London following Napoleon's defeat simply by wearing an elaborate moustache at a time when face fashion remained smooth. The Regency Dandies had never seen anything quite like it, and von Blücher set a trend amongst military men of a certain rank that defined them thereafter.

Another German, Prince Albert, was perhaps instrumental in popularising the old upper-lip 'hairy bogie' during his high-profile stint as appendage to Queen Victoria. By the middle of the 19th century, moustaches were becoming visible and fashionable adornments on the male countenance; and even if they weren't, gargantuan whiskers certainly were. Then the beard – for so long a symbol either of idleness or insanity in England – began to sprout on the chins of the powerful and influential. By the back end of the Victorian era, beards had blossomed into huge bushy beasts – impenetrable pubic forests that made every proud owner look ten years older and ten stone heavier.

These thick, dense thickets of fuzz could be worn by everyone from a sporting hero of the masses like the cricketer WG Grace or the age's great scientific mind Charles Darwin. Indeed, it's hard to think of an eminent Victorian bereft of a beard; a big beard appeared to signify the virility of Empire and the imperial supremacy of the British. On a more frivolous level, the legacy of von Blücher was also expanded upon as we entered the Edwardian era, when extravagant moustaches re-emerged more outrageously flamboyant than ever – the kind later to be seen under the noses of Jimmy

Edwards and Sir Gerald Nabarro as a means of distinguishing both from the spotless visages of their contemporaries.

The final Prime Minister whose face was framed by an archetypal Victorian beard was the Marquess of Salisbury, who left No.10 in 1902 (though we may have a more austere example of the beard renting the property soon - if nobody has confidence in Boris, that is). The last PM to have merely a moustache was Harold Macmillan; he may have stepped down from office in the year that Beatlemania broke, but Supermac had earned his spurs in the distant trenches. Indeed, if we take a rare look at the First World War in purely aesthetic terms, it's interesting to note how heavy facial hair was one of the minor casualties of the carnage. As a consequence, the Roaring 20s were largely clean-shaven, with the pencil-thin moustache being the sole concession to the former masculine trademark.

For around half-a-century, the beard retreated into a kind of shadowy cult existence; often, it implied an intellectual elitism, usually worn by academics, playwrights or earnest folkies. There was a mini-revival among students inspired by both the fad for 'Trad Jazz' and the charismatic firebrand Fidel Castro at the turn of the 1960s; but the beard didn't really return to the faces of the young on a wider scale until the end of the decade. Once The Beatles gave notice to the Mop Top era by growing moustaches, the razor blade was suddenly downgraded as an essential item in every gentleman's bathroom cabinet.

Amongst the numerous variations on offer in the hirsute hippie era, the Zapata had its moment – eventually becoming synonymous with such contrasting icons of the age as Peter Wyngarde and David Crosby – whereas the beard came to be regarded as an indication of revolutionary radicalism whilst also regaining its old quasi-religious symbolism, as seen on both Maharishi and Manson. By the beginning of the 70s, however, the ubiquitous beard was much as home on the effete chin of an Open University lecturer as it was on the huge blubbery jawline of Giant Haystacks. Even the defiantly androgynous Glam Rock had an unlikely beardie-weirdy in the shape of the larger-than-life Roy Wood.

Post-Punk, the beard represented the old guard as much as the gatefold sleeve of a Yes concept album, and the 1980s was relatively hairless as far as the face went; not until the 'designer stubble' craze at the end of the decade did young men looked upon as style icons feel brave enough to forego a shave again. The breakdown of the rigid rules and regulations governing the length of hair and the height of hemlines that began in the 90s (and has continued to this day) probably happened because popular culture finally reached a point where everything had been done before and there was nothing new left to say; suddenly, we entered a pick 'n' mix age in which the distinctive looks of recent decades could coexist simultaneously, albeit all stripped of their original context. The reappearance of the beard on young chins certainly wasn't accompanied by a revival of the tribal significance it had possessed in the 60s; then again, nothing in the culture had tribal significance anymore.

Some men who grow a beard keep it for life – I'd never have known an uncle of mine hadn't been born with one until I saw a photo of him in his clean-shaven youth, for example; others try it, don't like it, and never try it again. I myself have never been drawn to it; sideburns are as far as I venture into that area, and being aware of their occasional itchiness makes me wonder how Hipsters or Imams manage to avoid their facial fungus becoming not only a nest for nibbling mites, but a repository for scraps of snacks. Not sure how women feel when their bearded men are amorous, though I should imagine the bushier breed are maybe preferable to the bristly brand; anyone whose stubbly father inflicted 'chinny pie' on them as a child could possibly have developed an understandably lifelong aversion to the latter. Women are remarkably adaptable to the individual image whims of their menfolk, however.

As far as most are concerned, a beard today symbolises little at all because its wearers are so varied. It can be worn by humourless Indie musicians, New Age gurus, ex-boy band members seeking to be taken seriously, movie stars aiming to prove their thespian mettle, slovenly students, old hippies, young hippies, and fat dads of both the urban and suburban variety. It has been, like every other fashion accessory of the last fifty years that began as a statement, utterly assimilated into the culture so that any sighting of one induces nothing more than a shrug of the shoulders and a 'whatever'. Amazing how many paragraphs the subject can generate during the silly season, mind...

IN THE BEGINNING WAS THE WORDSMITH
2 September 2019

Around three years ago, this here blog inadvertently began to take on the shape of a broadsheet obituary section; a remarkable number of famous names fell like dominos in a short space of time and each had made a significant enough mark on me to warrant my noting their passing in a post. No idea what was in the water in 2016, but the legends that shuffled off this mortal coil at the time would've been better advised not to drink it. Anyhow, the pace of passing away thankfully seems to have slowed down since then and I only feel compelled to devote a post to the loss of an important figure now if they'd contributed in some shape or form to the person I am today. Bearing in mind what I do for 'a living', there's no way I can let this day go by without paying tribute to Terrance Dicks.

Now, whilst I appreciate his is not a name universally acknowledged, to those in the know – and whose childhoods existed in that surreal cultural bubble called the 1970s – Terrance Dicks was an alchemist of the imagination as much as Lewis Carroll or Kenneth Grahame had been to previous generations. Not only was he 'Doctor Who' script-editor during one of the programme's greatest purple patches (from 1968-74); he also authored the essential novelisations of the show's stories that were the only method of reliving them or visiting them for the first time in a pre-VHS, DVD and On-Demand era. The first-ever 'proper' book I read that didn't have more pictures than words in it was penned by Dicks – 'Doctor Who and the Web of Fear'; I wrote my first-ever 'proper' book after reading it. Terrance Dicks therefore prised open doors to me that have remained at the very least ajar ever since.

Denied the means of replaying favourite episodes of 'Doctor Who' over and over again on a screen, children of the 70s had no choice but to replay them in their heads – something that would have been considerably more difficult had not Dicks painted the Time Lord's landscape with such vivid and dynamic descriptive expertise. Free from the restraints of a BBC budget, the worlds the Doctor visited (and the creatures that inhabited them) could be visualised on the page of a Target paperback in ways today's younger fans can't possibly comprehend. As much as I would've loved to have been able to access any Jon Pertwee or Tom Baker adventure on TV whenever I felt like it as an eight-year-old, looking back I'm glad I couldn't. What the novelisations did was to really facilitate the means to re-imagine them, means that have enabled me to see other worlds and inhabit other imaginary lives from then on, not to mention creating my own – something I couldn't have done had not Terrance Dicks showed me how.

After co-writing a handful of episodes of 'The Avengers' in the late 60s, Terrance Dicks joined the scriptwriting team on 'Doctor Who' at a point when the series was faltering in the ratings and beginning to seem as though it had run its course. The exhausting work schedule for all involved in a show that was almost on all-year round (in the manner of a soap) pushed the Second Doctor Patrick Troughton into retiring from the role, and with British television's monochrome era coming to a close, many figured 'Doctor Who' would be just another casualty of the change into colour. Dicks had other ideas. When Dicks was promoted to script-editor, Barry Letts took over as producer and the combination of their respective talents saved the series; the inspired casting of Jon Pertwee undoubtedly played a major part in the transformation of the show's fortunes, but the men behind the scenes were the ones who rerouted the direction of the programme and took it to unprecedented heights of popularity and success.

The Doctor was now exiled to earth by the Time Lords, which was handy on account of the increase in alien invasions of the south-east poised to take place. With the Tardis temporarily out of action, he was forced to work alongside a military organisation called UNIT; specialising in the unexplained, UNIT was led by Brigadier Lethbridge-Stewart, a character played in consummate officer-class style by Nicholas Courtney; the 'Brig' became the Watson to the Doctor's Holmes. Letts & Dicks then thought it right the pair should have a Moriarty, so they created the character of The Master, played with sinister charisma by Roger Delgado. Augmented by female sidekicks such as Katy Manning's Jo Grant and

Elisabeth Sladen's Sarah-Jane Smith, the UNIT 'family' provided the Doctor and the viewer with a solid foundation for repelling the forces of evil and proved a winning formula throughout Dicks' tenure as script-editor.

Dicks also assembled a formidable team of talents to pen the stories that enraptured millions every Saturday teatime; the likes of Terry Nation, Malcolm Hulke, Robert Holmes, Robert Sloman, Bob Baker and Dave Martin may have severely tested the patience of set designers and monster manufacturers in Shepherd's Bush, but they gave children with latent imaginations permission to imagine. Some of us have never stopped imagining.

After five years at the helm, Letts & Dicks decided to time their departure with that of Jon Pertwee; but just as the leading man passed on the baton to an actor who pushed the bar even higher, the most successful double act in the programme's history to date handed over to Philip Hinchcliffe and Robert Holmes, confident the series was in very safe hands indeed – which it was. After writing the adventure that inaugurated the Tom Baker era, Terrance Dicks finally left 'Doctor Who', though in a way he never really did. Not only did he contribute a further handful of stories to the show in the late 70s, but his authorship of over 60 of the Target 'Doctor Who' novelisations through the remainder of the 70s and into the 80s ensured his involvement with the series remained a source of income as well as a means of regularly exercising his storytelling talents. He later became a permanent fixture on the generous extras accompanying the DVD releases of 'Who' adventures from his era.

If, like me, your time at school was more a case of learning how to survive a beating than learning, the inspirational teacher archetype as portrayed by Robin Williams in 'Dead

Poets' Society' or Richard Griffiths in 'The History Boys' was pure fiction. You therefore had to find that inspiration elsewhere, looking to individuals operating in other arenas to fire the imagination and stoke the curiosity for genuine education. Television was once abundant in such towering tutors: James Burke in the field of science, David Attenborough in natural history, and – through his stewardship of 'The South Bank Show' – Melvyn Bragg in the Arts. When it came to an introduction to the written word, for me Terrance Dicks played that part. I've travelled far and wide in terms of that word since, but I wouldn't have been on such an invigorating journey had not Dicks packed my rucksack with paperbacks and sent me on my way. I owe him.

THE SOLITARY LIFE
7 September 2019

When I was a kid, the only people I knew who lived on their own were a few old ladies. I assumed they were all widows, going by the sepia-tinted portraits of Brylcreemed young men I sometimes spied on the sideboard. They probably lost their husbands in the war; but if they were of actual pensionable age (rather than merely 'looking old', as anyone over-40 did back then), I guess some of them might have been widowed in the '14-18 bash as much as the sequel. It was a long time ago. I was given the impression the solitary life was reserved for a very narrow demographic; there was nobody in my wider family who lived on their own, for example. Aunts and uncles already out of their teens remained at home until they got married; that was presented to me as the natural order of things. None of them went to university either, so they didn't even get to experience what now seems to be the routine route to liberation – even if returning to the nest as a debt-addled graduate with little hope of being a homeowner is the inevitable anticlimax to this adolescent interregnum.

Unlike my childhood, those who live on their own today aren't necessarily ageing widows, and being the sole resident of one's abode is no longer viewed as especially unusual or even a little suspect if you don't resemble Ena Sharples or Minnie Caldwell. A 16% increase in the number of Brits living alone in the 20 years between 1997 and 2017 pushed the numbers up to 7.7 million; and whilst widows and widowers naturally still figure, higher divorce rates have played their part too; what used to be referred to as spinsters and bachelors are also far more abundant today than they were 40-odd years ago.

Interestingly, whilst there has been a 16% fall in the 25-44 age groups, the 45-64 demographic has seen a rise of 53%, with a higher proportion of both the divorced and the never-married filling the stats, reflecting changing social mores. Men living alone outnumber women – particularly in the 25-34 groups – until we reach the 55-64 groups, when the numbers even themselves out. The former groups mostly consist of the unmarried, whereas divorcees dominate the latter. All age groups, however, are less likely to own their home than married couples without children. Rented accommodation in later life can bring with it specific uncertainties and insecurities; higher levels of anxiety and lower levels of happiness are also attributed to living alone when compared to couples.

Of course, being alone doesn't necessarily equate with being lonely; as Bryan Ferry once so memorably said, 'loneliness is a crowded room'. Indeed, for every Eleanor Rigby, there is someone quite content to own their own space, especially if they've experienced an unhappy marriage or have made a conscious choice to avoid matrimony altogether. One's profession can also play a part in the success of one's living arrangements; some jobs are conducive to domestic bliss, whereas others encompass antisocial hours or are simply designed for solitude. I can certainly vouch for the latter. Unless writers could work out a way to 'jam' in the manner musicians do – perhaps sitting in a circle hammering away at their laptops in synch – it's very much something that is allergic to the communal and enhanced by the absence of company.

The creative process can last days, weeks and sometimes months, during which time a writer must be the least desirable spouse it's possible to imagine. Married men-of-the-pen who managed to make a handsome living from it have at least enjoyed the luxury of a 'writing shed' at the bottom of the garden; both Dickens and Roald Dahl famously retreated to theirs when the muse struck, and their families understood this meant 'do not disturb'. Rented flats on the top floors of houses aren't quite as accommodating, though at least the solitary life in such circumstances ensures that which Virginia Woolf famously referred to as 'a room of one's own.'

Naturally, for every plus to living alone there is a minus. Whilst there are many solitary dwellers whose boy/girlfriends regularly sleep over and therefore enjoy a 'part-time' relationship that can work for both parties, there are plenty more bereft of that option. If one has nobody to come home to of an evening or wake up with in the morning, the opportunities to self-indulge in self-abuse (and I'm not talking strictly masturbation) are myriad. With nobody to watch over you or rein in your excesses, the temptation to overdo it can be tempting indeed. The problem is, unlike being an overgrown Macaulay Culkin, the novelty of the home alone scenario ceases to be a novelty if it's the norm. It's easy to slip into the mindset that nobody gives a shit, so why should you; and that's a hard habit to break, one that fuels such self-indulgence. Drugs are a popular passport to personal oblivion;

but when it comes to writers, the demon drink appears to be the most common excuse for not knowing when to stop.

Although a considerable stretch from being a 'proper alcoholic', I admit that until relatively recently I was well on my way to having a serious drink problem; and what had initially emerged as a psychological crutch following a personal tragedy quickly morphed into the clichéd components of the author's armoury. I completely fell for the stereotype of the death-wish wordsmith with the bottle of scotch and packet of fags as his constant companions and suffered the consequences in terms of the damage it does to those around you. When I belatedly recognised the damage it was doing to *me,* I finally did something about it – even though I left it far too late to salvage what it had already cost me. My stint as Ray Milland interestingly had no adverse effect on the work – which probably made it easier to avoid addressing the issue – but its slow-burning impact on my life beyond the written word was devastating.

I can take a less-than nourishing crumb of comfort from the fact I was a 'funny' drunk rather than nasty (like my father) or violent (like those found in Saturday city centres); but it's not much in the way of solace when I reflect on what a selfish, nihilistic dickhead I was. In truth, I am profoundly ashamed of the way I behaved and no apology to the injured party can ever be good enough. But at least I've narrowed down my consumption from an average daily intake of two bottles of wine, a dozen glasses of whisky and half-a-bottle of vodka to a solitary Chardonnay one evening a week. I might drink it wholly alone, but at least it's all I drink.

Food can be another casualty of the solitary life. The appeal of a hearty meal doesn't necessarily escape those living alone, but the lengthy preparation can feel like an immense demand on both time and energy when there's only one mouth to feed; the easy alternative of some microwaveable plastic that can be unsealed, heated and scoffed in barely five minutes reflects the fact that solitude sometimes breeds hostility towards the ceremonies reserved for couples. In contrast to the instant meal for one, preparing, cooking, stirring and serving a proper dinner for two is a ritual that can span an hour or more, albeit a ritual that – if shared – can be as exquisitely intimate an experience as any that two people can enjoy with their clothes on.

Living on your own, as with sharing your life, has the potential to be either a blessing or a curse depending on the circumstances; both arrangements have their advantages as well as disadvantages, and both should be tried at least once. I've known many a miserable soul trapped in a loveless relationship, just as I've known many a life and soul for whom the thought of having to share their space is anathema. Ironically, when one examines the statistics, one is very much not alone in being alone.

3

It was a very bad year

Posts from the edge

I suppose some of you regulars may have started to wonder where I'd gone. The brutal truth is I just can't write at the moment. I'm only pushing myself to write this because I feel I owe you for your loyalty over the past couple of years. This week, I experienced a bereavement that has utterly numbed me and completely killed the urge to compose. I can't offer any sort of take on the remaining weeks of this vile, wretched year and the last thing I can face right now is the thought of having to relive it by reviewing it. Even if I tried, the end result would be so bilious and bleak that it'd make the last-but one post read like a jolly holiday brochure. You may have noticed a more cynical and pessimistic edge creeping into recent posts, anyway; I didn't want this to become a permanent trend or a defining characteristic of a blog I've always tried to enliven with gallows humour as my hand is on my heart and my tongue is in my cheek.

Some might say carrying on regardless by churning out sardonic articles about something in the news every day could serve as a convenient distraction; to be honest, the most time an average post takes to write isn't much more than a couple of hours, anyway, so it's not as if the exercise is especially taxing. But if all you feel like doing is raging at the world in a relentless tide of negativity, it would quickly grate with the reader; besides, if that's what the people are looking for, there's always Alex Jones' YT channel.

At the moment, anything I even attempted to write would just be too depressing, too despondent and, frankly, *too much* – not just for you, but me too. Away from online discourse, I've even broken a previously-unbroken habit of 13 years, that of writing a private diary entry every night before bedtime, because I can't face documenting the day's events anymore.

I won't inflict any of this on you, so I'll be taking a break for a bit. Right now, I definitely doubt I'll add another post to 2017's long list, and I can't say with any degree of accuracy when normal service will be resumed. Bidding good riddance to 2017 implies 2018 will be welcomed with open arms, but I'm certainly not looking forward to 2018 because I simply can't see it being an improvement on the twelve months we've just endured. As far as I'm concerned, it'll probably be even worse. It's hard to envisage anything remotely positive up ahead, which does somewhat reduce the likelihood of posts that might put a smile on your face. And I don't want to dwell on how much I'm hurting because it could easily translate as self-pity, like 'All By Myself' on a bloody loop – the Celine Dion cover. Imagine that.

For two years on the Telegram and perhaps around the same amount of time on another (now-defunct) blog that I reckon most of you here can recall, I've been a busy bee and haven't paused to catch my breath for more than two or three days at a time. In the end, I may find that two or three days more than that away from the blog might rekindle the compulsion to pick up where I left off and I could be back within a week; but I don't feel that way today. I feel burnt out. Maybe a longer sabbatical than I've so far taken really will help to recharge my jaded batteries. Who knows? I'm not intending to call it a day completely. Even though it has brought me zilch financial riches, writing's all I can really do and I generally can't stop myself from doing it. With that in mind, I suppose it's inevitable I'll return as long as I feel I'm wanted.

For many, the majority of life is lived in a monochrome Kansas that is made tolerable by brief glimpses of

Technicolor Oz. It should be the other way round, but it never seems to be, alas. Kicks in the teeth are commonplace, body blows par for the course. It sucks. And it doesn't matter how hard you work and how many hours you put in, the rewards are usually conspicuous by their absence. When/if that rare moment of magic called happiness comes along, for God's sake grab it, cherish it, and always remember just how precious it truly is; never take it for granted; it can be painfully transient, and when it's gone it'll rip your heart out.

I don't think I'll have another opportunity to say it, but thanks for your constant support, and have a good Christmas if you can. After all, in the end, the love you take is equal to the love you make.

IT'S BEEN A LONG, COLD LONELY WINTER
6 May 2018

How fatal taking for granted the loyalty and devotion of one's audience can be was never better illustrated than in the swift falling from favour of the poor old Bay City Rollers. Almost omnipotent in 1975, the nice-but-dim young Scotsmen were the UK's belated home-grown answer to The Osmonds. Possessing the clean-cut boy-next-door appeal guaranteed to send nascent female hormones into the same overdrive as Utah's most famous family firm had done, the rise of the Rollers dramatically served to usurp the Mormon musical missionaries. Prompted by their astronomical British success, the Rollers then looked to replicate it on the other side of the Atlantic – despite the fact this had already proven to be a futile exercise for immediate pop predecessors like Marc Bolan and Slade. Yet the Rollers got off to the best possible start when 'Saturday Night' shot to the top of the Billboard Hot 100 at the beginning of 1976, an achievement that naturally booked them on the next flight to America.

But the timing of the Rollers' Stateside expedition was especially unfortunate. In 1976, two emerging musical genres that would go on to dominate what remained of the 70s – Punk and Disco – were luring away sizeable chunks of the pop audience from the hormonal cauldron of the teenybop arena; at the same time, those unmoved by Donna Summer or The Sex Pistols were mesmerised by a certain self-contained Swedish hit-machine. Rollermania was also destined to be a temporary phenomenon – a necessary rites-of-passage ritual for teenage girls before boyfriends and babies, as well as being the last hysterical hurrah of a frenzied trend that defined the decade until it grew up and moved on. The band returned home from what turned out to be a short-lived stint in the American spotlight to find their audience diminished and the *zeitgeist* having relocated; they never scored another No.1.

However random or irrelevant this brief detour into the reassuringly safe refuge of pop culture history might appear to be, it is my roundabout way of making a point. Deciding to tentatively return to a medium I had no choice but to plunge into suspended animation five months ago might make it appear as though I reckon it's 'business-as-usual' and we pick up where we left off in December. As much as it flatters my ego to imagine it, I'm aware that assuming all regular commentators and readers have spent every day of 2018 so far scanning their inbox first thing on a morning in the hope of seeing a notification informing them a new 'Winegum Telegram' post has appeared – and their days therefore being ruined as a consequence of this not coming to pass – is utterly absurd. Yes, I'm conscious kind comments have continued to periodically pepper the blog during the hiatus; but to envisage lives revolving around the proclamations of Chairman Petunia, and collapsing into complementary stasis in the absence of them, is a conceit even I would never countenance.

How do I explain why coming back to this has been so difficult? Oh, well – think of string and the length of it. Perhaps it's been so difficult because 'gifts' that previously provided satisfaction and a sense of purpose (if an absence of income) lost their collective value for me. Experiencing a severe dent to self-confidence re my 'creative capabilities' was one reason for ruling out a return; recent reunions with old posts on here - read for the first time with real detachment - left me impressed albeit simultaneously disbelieving I'd written them. Yes, each element is connected and affected. One particularly devastating bombshell can have a big enough impact to bleed into every facet of one's life, even areas that have no direct relation to it, triggering a chain reaction that can leave one pretty bloody winded. Until the event that knocked me for six, I could write a post for this, put a jolly little satirical video together for YouTube, and maybe even work on a novel – all in a day's work. And now, everything has either slowed to a snail's pace or ground to a complete halt, which is a crippling state of affairs for someone whose identity is defined by his creativity; this is actually the first prose I've written since December.

Noting regular references to depressive bouts in past posts, I feel almost envious of the author's naivety, realising I had no real idea how low I could go; but even someone with 'previous' isn't prepared for the kind of emotional meltdown I've undergone, and Nietzsche's assertion that 'if you stare long enough into the abyss, the abyss will stare back at you' has been an unwelcome guest at my dinner table of late.

Don't think I haven't noticed news stories that I would no doubt have penned plenty posts about had I still been active; but being relieved of my duties has spared me extended exposure to items that would only have added to my unhealthy state of mind had I had to immerse myself in them via the compositional process. The necessity of such survival tactics means I've allowed the opening months of 2018 to pass me by in a way I never have with a year before; but I've been powerless to prevent my paralysing inertia. Having said that, I did manage to condense many of these headlines into one video a month or so ago, which felt like a small step in the right direction; it says what I felt needed to be said without having to devote a dozen posts to the subjects featured, so it was a tiny triumph of sorts.

Even with the invaluable support of close friends, however (many of whom have revealed touching depths of understanding and empathy), I remain frustratingly entrenched in a Groundhog Day distinctly lacking colour or joy and where the only thing I've been able to detect around the corner is a bloody great brick wall, forcing me to adopt the 'one day at a time' approach to life – one bereft of forward planning and predictions, though also, mercifully, devoid of Lena Martell's greatest hit (Sweet Jesus).

During the darkest sections of this extremely dark tunnel, the only contemporary cultural artefact that seemed capable of holding my attention was BBC4's French police series, 'Spiral' – and that was mainly because any wavering from the subtitles would bugger-up the plot, so I had no alternative but to concentrate. Otherwise, unable to focus for long on a book, I lost myself in a steady diet of DVDs that provided nostalgic comfort food for the head as well as solid no-nonsense drama that has stood up remarkably well 40 years on. Give 'The Sandbaggers' a try if you enjoy old-school Cold War espionage in the le Carré mode; one of you out there already has – that much I do know (according to the latest memo from C, anyway). Similarly, a superb album of eccentric curios and buried treasure unearthed by St Etienne's Bob Stanley and Pete Wiggs titled 'English Weather' got me through the winter on a loop, whereas Joni Mitchell at her mid-70s peak is easing me through the spring. Only wish these healing hands could carry me back to where I was before I needed them; but they can't.

Knowing not if this post is one-night stand or series reboot, I can't guarantee when the next one will be; but architectural historian Jonathan Glancey's reflection on the sad descent of architectural critic Ian Nairn into drunken disillusionment and an all-too premature end feels relevant. 'If you do fight continually against the things that make you angry,' he said, 'you get exhausted...exhausted in your mind, exhausted in your heart, and exhausted in your soul.' Modesty prevents me from placing my own humble kicks against the pricks in the same league as Nairn's poetic tirades aimed at architects and town-planners from the 50s to the 70s – tirades that graced the pages of national newspapers and networked TV screens. I do recognise a kindred spirit when I see one, however. Symptoms of Nairn's downfall seem uncomfortably familiar as well, which is why any return to regular writing on here has to be motivated by a genuine compulsion to do it (rather than a misguided sense of obligation), believing I *can* do it, and being convinced people actually want to read it.

So, that's the best I can do right now. You heard it here first. Okay. Until we meet again...soon, I hope...

PETUNIA PITSTOP
24 May 2018

Overwhelmed by both a sudden injection of big-budget big bucks and the exotic distraction of tax-saving excursions to tax-haven locations, John Lennon famously reflected on the change in cinematic circumstances during the filming of 'Help!', the second Beatles movie. Strumming away in the

Technicolor upgrade of the Bahamas, Lennon wryly remarked, 'I'm an extra in me own film.' Well, I'm making my second cameo appearance on my own blog since December, and I'm afraid I'm only passing through again. The kind words and encouraging response to the last post may have failed to elicit a written reply on my part, but all comments were much appreciated, as were the numerous re-tweets by long-term supporters. It's nice to feel loved, virtually or not.

Before I go any further, I apologise. This was never intended to be – and indeed, never *has* been – one of those blogs that exist solely as a narcissistic outlet for an author assuming his or her life is as fascinating to the readership as it is to him or herself. I'd hate for this instalment to be regarded as the point at which a blog with an unlimited remit shrank into a narrow sequence of hastily scrawled postcards from the edge. I'm trying my best not to make this a regular habit, honest.

Of course, just as a novelist's autobiographical journey tends to infiltrate the back story of their lead character (however hard they fight against it), identification with the subject matter under discussion on here has regularly led to vague asides – or more explicit references – to my own back story. Even a piece I wrote about the Israel/Palestine thing a year or two ago (I forget when) was given a little more emotional substance with the tale of my Uncle Joe and this long-gone figure's membership of the Palestine Police in the years leading up to 1948; ditto the revelation of the family lineage linking me to the Enola Gay's flight over Hiroshima in 1945. I suppose it's only natural that many of the news stories to have caught my eye and provoked a post are stories I've made some connection with, thus (hopefully) elevating them above simple journalistic reportage, of which there is already more than enough out there.

I know this hasn't always happened; plenty posts have simply been vociferous responses to events that have angered or infuriated me, fuelled by nothing *more* than anger or fury. And, it goes without saying, there's always the mischievous spirit of satire on stand-by to intervene when the ludicrousness of politics – identity or otherwise – has risen its daft head yet again. Having said that, whenever my own life experience or that of friends and lovers has bled into a post with a wider surface context, I personally feel I've usually managed to get the balance right (as Depeche Mode once observed) and have successfully steered clear of self-indulgence.

To return to the second paragraph, I don't believe my life *is* especially fascinating – though I will concede, however, that being able to view it with a degree of out-of-body detachment helps me 'manage' it. Watching a decline and fall through the mirror is undeniably unhealthy, yet curiously compelling in the same way one's gaze can never be entirely averted from the bouncy genitals of a streaker. You can't help but look, despite yourself. The fact is I tend to interpret life experience as material for 'Art' (no less pretentious word was available, alas), and I'm talking both good *and* bad life experience. In the case of the latter, it's the kind of thing that makes uncomfortable reading for those who know me; but as I only appear capable of coping with crises if I respond to them with pen, paper or keyboard, there's no alternative in the great battle for survival. I'm certainly not enjoying scrabbling around for tiny fragments of hope down here at Rock Bottom Central, but I do feel as though my life is out of my hands right now and I just have to deal with it in the only way I can – until the day comes when I'm in control again.

If it is true that dwellers of an urban environment are never more than six feet away from a rat, it feels right now as though I'm never more than six *minutes* away from remembering recent events that led me to where I currently reside – no book, music, movie or TV show can remove that from the room. Therefore, reading, listening and viewing habits work in empathetic conjunction with the mood of the moment. It's no contradiction that sad songs speak loudest to us when we're sad; the last thing we need when feeling like shit is being ordered to get up and boogie. Moreover, it's both amazing and comforting that the most trusted voices to have serenaded the listener throughout adult life have something to say for every occasion. Indeed, we are reassured when the voices that have been there for us when times are good are also there for us when times aren't; and we know we're not alone when our friends sing of suffering. Just listen to Marvin Gaye's contribution to 1974's 'You Are Everything', an otherwise gooey duet with Diana Ross; when he sings 'Oh-whoa, darling/I just can't go on, living life as I do/comparing each girl with you/knowing they just won't do/they're not you', you know he's not only been there, but he's bought the company that made the T-shirt in true Victor Kiam fashion.

Silly YouTube videos may well be the babies I nonchalantly dump in children's homes once I've popped them out, but they make some people happy and – for the moment – they are serving a useful purpose that other outlets currently aren't. They are in no way a pointer to revived spirits, merely a means of keeping idle hands away from the Devil's gaze. Nevertheless, they have survived unscathed and perhaps act as an unexpected manifestation of the obstinate resilience we all seem able to produce when confronted by our deepest fears. Hell, I'll take whatever I can get.

Sometimes, however, the smallest, most innocuous interventions make a difference. Old Mother Cable may conveniently sidestep his shameful role in the scandalous selling-off of the Royal Mail as he attempts to big-up the latest Lib Dem 'revival' by posing as a political moral barometer; but the postman (or woman, in my case) can still deliver the goods in the face of privatised indifference to the customer. Anonymous surprises through the letter-box can momentarily put the brakes on any recourse to Alanis Morrissette when the helplessness of the dispossessed is desperately seeking a soundtrack; and the anonymous have nothing to fear. I may be a wounded animal, but that animal isn't a dragon. All this proves is that, whilst the systems with which we make contact may be myriad in this century, the oldest (well, after smoke signals and carrier pigeons) hits the mark even now, despite Vince's best bloody efforts.

I shan't bore you with further details, though – oblique or otherwise. Yes, I'd like to get back to the wider world and escape the confines of the internal compound (trust me, it's crap in here); but it ain't easy, however many open goals the media leaves on my doorstep. Bear with me if you can and I'll try to phone home again next time I've got some spare change.

THROUGH THE PAST, DARKLY
6 June 2018

Grinning and bearing my way through precisely six months of paralysis following the abrupt stopping of the clocks last December has had a funny effect on my perception of time. Frozen as both participant and observer, one way of suppressing a sense of uselessness at my sudden inability to respond to contemporary events in the customary manner has been to retreat into a digitally restored version of the past. After all, when circumstances rob you of the present and deprive you of a future in the process (or at least the future you thought you were getting), the one certainty you can turn to is the past, a place where the ground beneath your feet is reassuringly solid.

This is a painless post in terms of writing (and, one hopes, reading); it's simply me taking a stress-free diversion into my viewing habits of the last half-year, one that may strike the odd chord merely as an entertaining interlude. And, as it's not unusual for this blog to mine a bit of nostalgia from archive telly, I speak today of 'Special Branch', a series produced by ITV back in the days when it added up to a good deal more as a broadcaster than the vacuous vacuum it currently inhabits. It's a series that has also provided me with a convenient distraction from recent events via the DVD box-set.

Originally a dramatic, franchise-justifying product of the fledgling Thames Television, 'Special Branch' first appeared at the fag-end of the monochrome era in late 1969. Starring the chunky-faced Derren Nesbitt as DCI Jordan, the series dramatised the middle man between CID and the Secret Service at the height of post-Philby Cold War paranoia. Nesbitt's Jordan was a flash young buck whose startlingly dapper dress sense always made him look as if he'd just stepped off a gentleman's fashion shoot for 'Town' magazine; a bit of a flamboyant oddity in stale environs populated by both stuffy Whitehall suits and crusty Met veterans, Jordan nevertheless got results as well as gorgeous 'dollies' resplendent in the big hair/false eyelashes/micro-dress ensembles popularised by the likes of Bobbie Gentry at the time.

Constantly thwarted by MI5 mandarin Moxon (played with slimy languor by Morris Perry), DCI Jordan eventually threw his career away when the seductive charms of recurring double-agent Christine Morris (the Bobbie Gentry blueprint *par excellence*) proved a little *too* seductive. But then, Jordan was very much a man of his time - a time when men weren't marginalised by a media intent on portraying the male of the species (and his 'toxic masculinity') as the embodiment of all evil whilst simultaneously wondering why so many examples of this useless, redundant relic end up jumping off rooftops.

Like most British drama of the era, 'Special Branch' in its original format was divided between studio sets shot on videotape and location inserts shot on film. Occasionally, embryonic OB (Outside Broadcast) cameras were used for exteriors, but the blatantly artificial lighting and shaky visuals suggested the time was not yet right for its use as a regular system for anything beyond on-the-spot news reports. The more familiar contrast between studio VT and location film was industry standard then and only seems jarring decades after the event, as does an acting style informed more by theatre than cinema. However, it clearly irked some working in TV and eventually led to the aesthetic rebirth of the show following a two-year hiatus in 1973.

Euston Films was established by Thames as a means of shooting serious, grown-up dramas entirely on film, both indoors and outdoors, and must have been a gritty innovation in the early 70s, particularly when compared to the slicker fantasy-adventure filmed series from the ITC stable. The revived 'Special Branch' was its first outing and it wasn't just the look of the series that had changed. The cast received a complete overhaul as well. Out had gone Detective Chief Inspector Jordan and his superior (played by Fulton Mackay long before he became a familiar face courtesy of a certain prisoner name of Norman Stanley Fletcher); in came the craggy countenance of DCI Alan Craven, played by George Sewell. Prior to his recruitment to the side of the good guys, Sewell had mostly been a character actor playing villains; he had a memorable role in 1971's seminal Brit gangster flick, 'Get Carter'. After 'Special Branch', he reverted to type; but in the part of Craven, Sewell excelled as a hard-boiled copper that the viewer could entirely believe in.

Considering the controversial role the actual Special Branch played in Northern Ireland in the 70s, the TV version of the department largely avoids such contentious areas and also distinguishes itself from its earlier incarnation by mostly steering clear of staple stories surrounding suspected spies and Marxist student revolutionaries. Often, the storylines seem suited to a series focusing on routine police work, though there are numerous 'firsts' present, not least the fact that the lead character has a girlfriend who happens to be black. Nobody would bat an eyelid at an interracial relationship today, but this was pretty groundbreaking stuff in 1973; in retrospect, the mixed-race love interest between Craven and a nurse called Pam is a refreshing development for mainstream drama and one that wasn't built upon for several years. Moreover, there's also the mental breakdown of a regular cast member, something which is handled with both surprising sensitivity and a welcome absence of 'issue'-led sentimentality so commonplace in present-day soaps.

The key ingredient in the reboot of 'Special Branch' is the introduction of the old cop/young cop dynamic when Patrick Mower appears as DCI Haggerty; initially a 'guest artist' (as the opening credits imply), Mower's arrogant and swaggering character is then bedded in as a permanent presence, providing the show with some testosterone bite and laying the foundations for the Regan & Carter double act of the series that ultimately succeeded it. Paul Eddington is also added in a pre-'Good Life' role as an MI5 bigwig whose urbane pomposity serves to frustrate the more hands-on approach of his subordinates on the street. The cast list is fleshed out by members of the wonderful rep company of character actors that peppers British TV drama of the 70s, some of whom eventually found leading roles of their own.

After two successful 'seasons' (as is now the norm to say), 'Special Branch' was dropped in favour of 'The Sweeney', a series produced by the same team, and one which took many elements from its predecessor but crucially cranked up the macho violence in the process. Thanks to consistent reruns from the early 80s onwards, the adventures of the Flying Squad have rarely been absent from our screens and have become established as the retrospective template for British police dramas, inspiring tributes as diverse as 'Life on Mars' and the memorable 'Comic Strip' homage, 'Detectives on the Verge of a Nervous Breakdown'. But none of that would have happened had not 'Special Branch' paved the way.

I don't know why, but an antiquated series produced in a different country has served a need almost half-a-century on for someone struggling to cope with the wasteland bequeathed to him, and has also opened a portal into a past far more alluring than anything the present can boast. An entirely irretrievable image of England, of course; but we all find our own personal panaceas when confronted by the unbearable. This has been mine – well, one of them. And when it comes to dealing with the troublesome twenty-first century, those of us who experienced at least thirty years of its predecessor can always count on its cultural artefacts to provide necessary shelter from the storm.

THE WAY WE LIVE NOW...AND THEN
23 June 2018

We may hate it, but advertising slogans can often linger. 'Say it with Flowers' said Interflora; and, as it happens, whenever I

181

think of Interflora, I think of Interpol. Perhaps the association stems from an obvious gag on something like 'The Two Ronnies'; many of their gags *were* obvious, but the obviousness of them was overridden by the comic charm of the performers. Anyway, where was I? Ah, yes, flowers – delivered to the doors of the consummated as well as the unrequited, sometimes motivated by guilt, sometimes by the need to remind someone you love them. They make an ideal house-warming gift, for example, when it comes to a new residence, being as they are the most potent symbols of rebirth and regeneration when love is in the air.

No, I'm NOT going to write about that shameless exhibitionist's manual known as 'Love Island'; besides, Nigel Kneale beat me to it by half-a-century with his unnervingly accurate satire on lowest-common-denominator twenty-first century television, 1968's 'The Year of the Sex Olympics'. This remarkable example of cultural soothsaying is one of the most uncanny crystal balls in TV history. If you haven't seen it, do; once you get over the occasionally theatrical acting and groovy 60s aesthetic impression of the future, the way in which it predicts the worst our goggle-box can offer today will evoke associations with everything from 'Castaway' and 'Big Brother' to the aforementioned STD-through-the-keyhole voyeur-fest on ITV2 and even the grotesque Smartphone suicide-watch trend. The dialogue – short, snappy and uncomfortably familiar in its irritating abbreviations – mirrors Orwell's belief in how language will eventually be narrowed and compressed into simple sound-bites. The ominous first words on-screen are 'Sooner than you think...'

The play's oft-stated division between the privileged and the rest ('High Drives' and 'Low Drives') inevitably evokes the Us and Them gap that the Brexit vote exposed; but to me it also anticipates the downgrading of one particular demographic in this country – one that is firmly rock bottom on the social scale fifty years later. A recent 'initiative' by a leading publisher that sought the input of unpublished authors made it clear who they were looking for. London-based, Oxbridge-educated chattering-class warriors burdened by the unbearable baggage of box-ticking have their preferred minorities to pat on the head and patronise, as novelist Lionel Shriver has bravely pointed out (much to her predictable Twitter crucifixion); and if you happen to emanate from a white working-class background free of further education, forget it. You are very much Low Drive – or 'Gammon', if you prefer; it's the insult it's OK to eat between meals without ruining your appetite.

For some, it matters not how many Sikhs are photographed with their arms round him, as Tommy Robinson's EDL past will always brand him a white supremacist; but both sides of the barricades have their own version of the truth and never the twain shall meet. Like similar headline-grabbing stunts by Peter Tatchell, the amateur *agent-provocateur* tactics of Robinson could be said to be looking for trouble and inviting arrest along with accompanying publicity. But maybe the climate requires such actions in order to receive any acknowledgment within media circles whose contempt for 'the Gammon' is evident to anyone bereft of blinkers. Somebody once proclaimed the face of Tommy Robinson will one day feature on a far-flung future bank-note. Another agitator called Thomas – the late Mr Paine – was similarly derided and demonised in his day, yet is viewed rather differently two-hundred years later, so who knows what criteria the Bank of England will employ when it comes to its cover stars of the twenty-second century? A shame Nigel Kneale isn't around anymore. *He* probably would.

Another fortune-teller called Karl Marx apparently said 'The more you have, the less you are' – a good point if applied to those who measure their worth by the number of material goods they possess; but how is that statement interpreted by the collectivism that contemporary Marx disciples espouse, especially in the Labour Party? I've always been averse to collectives, instinctively recoiling from their 'block vote' rhetoric; I'm too much of an individual, never a team player. If I'd been gifted with sporting prowess, I'd have been at home on the tennis court rather than the football pitch. The problem with collectivism is the compulsory sacrifice of the individual voice to the consensus, and that's just not me, Jeremy.

Jonathan Meades in his recent excellent BBC4 treatise on the uses and abuses of the English language spent a section dissecting the collectivist clichés that arise when eleven men play eleven more; but he primarily focused on the jargon employed by the Law, politics and business to mask true intentions in a tsunami of verbal diarrhoea that is deliberately intended to leave the Gammon crying 'My brain hurts!', therefore throwing him back into the primordial embrace of 'Love Island'. The sad fact is that this works because we allow it to, just as we allow one knee-jerk response to a pair of tits on a lifeboat-man's mug to damage the public standing of the RNLI, or we allow consensual sex to be reclassified as rape. Makes you proud to be British, doesn't it – whatever that means.

At one time, it could mean Noel Coward or Anthony Burgess; Margaret Rutherford or Terry Thomas; Tony Hancock or John Arlott; John Osborne or Quentin Crisp; Peter Sellers or Peter Cook; John Betjeman or John Lennon; Ian Nairn or Oliver Postgate. The Great British manufacturing industry wasn't merely about economics; it was also about individual voices –

all lost now to revisionist market forces. We don't make 'em like that anymore because we've been absorbed into the global village chain-store, flogged at half-price by a new breed of national shopkeepers.

Another neglected gem from the pen of the man who gave us 'The Year of the Sex Olympics' was an obscure anthology series produced by ATV called 'Beasts'; it's creepy in that unique way only 70s TV can be, set in a Britain when the moribund and the macabre meet. One story concerned a poltergeist in a supermarket, though not the kind of supermarkets we have now; it was a store owned by one of those small regional chains that no longer exist, like Hillard's or Vivo. Viewing this time capsule recently, I experienced a strange sensation of warmth as childhood brand names flew off the shelf at the height of the petulant spirit's rage. Rows of Ricicles probably wouldn't be within the poltergeist's sights today, no doubt censored by finger-wagging government guidelines on sugar intake - let alone a version featuring Florence and Dougal on the front of the box.

And so, restlessness forced me outdoors a month ago; I went for a meandering walk – and if you've made it to this paragraph you'll know by now I'm good at meandering. Unfortunately, simple exercise (physical or mental) no longer seems a valid enough reason to stroll alone. When I ended up on a local park, my aversion to collectives worked against me; I felt increasingly self-conscious re my sore thumb solo status, surrounded as I was by women and dogs. I had neither with me, though I came home to the ghosts of both. And cats. But I end where I began, thinking of flowers as potent symbols of rebirth and regeneration. Maybe I should get some. Life may now be a silver medal, but at least I can make it smell nice for a few days.

SEVEN AND THE RAGGED TIGER
6 July 2018

Seven is a highly potent number. It concluded the head-count for both dwarves and Samurai; it provided us with the seas, the deadly sins, the colours of the rainbow, the wonders of the ancient world and the ages of man. It gave us the right quota of brides for the right quota of brothers, the amount of years for a marital itch, the veils needed for Salome's erotic dance routine, the title of a disturbing 90s horror movie, Enid Blyton's secret alternative to her famous quintet, the necessary inches for the classic pop single, the correct collection of rogues for an intergalactic outlaw called Blake, and – of course – the assembled days of the week. It seems to have followed me around. I was born in a year ending in seven, lived at a No.7 for the best part of two decades, and my current home is a residence whose separate flat and house numbers add up to...you guessed it. And now I have seven months on the clock to measure my faltering progress through the brave new world I was dumped in as 2017 drew to a grim full stop.

Careful – I'm perilously close to a pattern so familiar on Twitter, that of relentlessly focusing on the one topic over and over again with mouth-frothing fanaticism. I never used to do that, but I never previously wrote for this blog whilst trying to recover from...er...well, a breakdown. No touchy-feely alternative word for it. I certainly don't want any of my jottings to be viewed as 'therapeutic' as a consequence, however. Even if trying to get back into the habit is undeniably a form of therapy for me, I should imagine coming to such posts as a reader when burdened with that awareness could make approaching them akin to a 'duty', precluding either enjoyment or stimulation and reducing the whole exercise to the reading equivalent of a professional goalkeeper allowing a special needs child to score a penalty for charity. I'm sure a holiday in Salisbury would seem more appealing right now.

OK, let's try to widen the picture a little by saying Brexit, Brexit, Brexit. Bored already, alas. Mind you, it *was* two years ago when we all made our way to the polling station and cast our vote, so should the subject still be the main headline day-after-never-ending-day? Tiresome doom 'n' gloom predictions abound on both sides if it does/doesn't turn out how either want it; and I'm afraid I've reached the point where I'm beginning to not care anymore. Most days, I feel as though this country is incurably f***ed anyway, but that's probably because on many of those days I feel as though *I'm* incurably f***ed. Sorry, it's not you; it's me.

I ain't no Jacob Rees-Mogg, extolling the economic virtues of Britain breaking with the EU whilst relocating my Russia-friendly business interests to Brussels-friendly Eire; and I ain't no Lord Adonis, wistfully waving goodbye to the Continent from the window-seat of a private plane flying over the Alps with a teary-eye that foresees endless referenda until the desirable result is achieved. At the same time, much like that gruesome twosome, mine is not an objective perspective right now – though I at least have the decency to leave the subject alone as a result.

I suppose I could indulge in the contemporary trend of anniversary-marking to fill otherwise empty column inches; it's not like I haven't before, after all. This year we've got 10 since the financial crash, 30 since Acid House, 50 since the Paris Spring, 70 since the birth of the NHS, and a century since women in the UK won the vote (well, as long as they were over 30). The latter two have received the most attention, with the NHS anniversary in particular plumbing a nauseating nadir of sentimental media waffle that has run parallel with - and appears contradicted by - the shocking revelations from Gosport and Chester. Mysteriously, very little coverage has been given to the impenetrable layers of self-interested and self-satisfied management swallowing up the bags of cash that governments routinely throw towards the NHS in the hope some of it will filter down to frontline nurses and patients. But I guess that doesn't fit the celebratory narrative.

Anyway, I'm not really paying attention. My much-missed feline companion passed away two years ago this month, yet just the other night the light caught one of her long-discarded nails embedded in the carpet – unseen since 2016. This tiny, seemingly insignificant fragment of a friend lost to me forever felt like an invaluable, precious gemstone when I excavated it; but any trinket touched by the lost keeps them close when we can no longer draw them to our breast. Some bin or burn such mementos because they cannot bear to be reminded; others find these articles imbued with a comforting resonance that serves as evidence they really *were* in our lives and we didn't imagine them. As someone once said, was it just a dream? Seemed so real to me.

But, what the hell! School's (almost) out for summer, so let's switch our attention to the World Cup and Wimbledon. Better that than allow our eyes to linger on ladies' legs and other exposed body parts lest we incur the wrath of those who permit female drooling over topless Aidan Turner whilst simultaneously condemning male longing to varnish the delicious porcelain flesh of Demelza with one's tongue. Long may her Cornish bosom heave, for drama is one of the Beeb's few remaining assets; by contrast, claims by the BBC's box-ticking 'comedy controller' that the Pythons wouldn't happen today because they were 'too white' gives an indication why the corporation's current comedic output is so dire. The sun must have gone to his diversity-mangled head.

I remember 1976, but it was different then; I did things in hot weather I can't do today. Besides, fun wasn't as 'organised' forty-two years ago as it is now; adult involvement in childhood summer pursuits was mercifully minimal. I feel fortunate to have had the freedom to climb trees, kick balls past woollen goalposts, and arrange toy soldiers for a pitched battle to the strains of 'Mars, the Bringer of War'. I steered clear of the Boy Scouts and the Cubs because I didn't want grown-ups imposing their twee, sanitised idea of fun upon me. Pity the poor monitored kids of 2018's heat-wave, who have never been left to their own devices and consequently can't entertain themselves.

No, the best thing about this time of year – if you burn the midnight oil, of course – is reluctantly retiring to bed around 3.00am and catching one last look at the world outside your window. The landscape still consists of silhouettes, but the sky isn't black; it's a luscious shade of blue that enables you to already discern the next day on the horizon, as though it were a great wave rolling towards you in slow motion, one that only matures into its finished form when it washes over you several hours later, stirring you from slumber in the process. That's a nice image to leave you with, at least. You don't need a weather-man to know which way the wind blows; but may you always have a tiger in your tank.

THE CLOWN DUELS
30 July 2018

Yeah, I'm back again for another isolated observation in my occasional series of 'Stars on 45'-style topical medleys. But while I might poke and prod a few minor irritants today, they essentially remain of a trivial nature to me; none of them irritate me enough to bring forth the froth to my mouth - unlike the subjects that fire the warring extremes on Twitter. One might almost imagine they have nothing else going on in their lives. Anyway, it felt right to endure one more unwelcome anniversary by stepping out of the shade for a few minutes; after all, if I leave this neglected baby of mine in the sun too long the poor whelp risks suffocation by spam - mostly in 'Russian' by the look of its distinctly Slavic appearance. By Jove, I'm being spied on!

God knows why I could possibly be of any interest to whatever name the KGB goes under these days, but it's moderately exciting to think I am. Maybe Vlad's online agitators think everyone here is pretending to be a 'Communist' now and they're curious. I'm as guilty as the next spoon when it comes to hankering after something before your own time simply because your own time is uninspiring and your perception of the time before your own has been shaped by something you read or a movie you saw. But it's a risky business. When one has no first-hand experience of something intriguing, it acquires a romantic allure and can be embraced without any awareness of its less attractive realities.

The latest fashion for proclaiming one's self a Communist is one that is only being followed by those with no personal memory of life behind the Iron Curtain. As far as irrelevant ideologies go, Communism is currently the fatuous political equivalent of a Ramones T-shirt, generally worn by people of an upbringing untroubled by hardship whose way of coping with guilt over their good fortune is to lecture those without it how they should live their lives. Each generation of Trotsky groupies cherry-picking Marx's greatest hits and compiling its own mix-tape knows what's best for the rest of us; and it's ironic that the current crop's default insult is to call their opponents Nazis when they themselves espouse a belief system responsible for more death and misery in the last century than even Adolf's mob managed.

Great in theory, terrible in practice, Communism's good intentions have been open to abuse from day one simply because the system makes it easier for the worst side of human nature to assert itself than even the far-from faultless Capitalism can boast. International sporting events being beamed into my childhood living room gave the names of now-defunct countries such as East Germany, Yugoslavia and Czechoslovakia an undeniably nostalgic ring – as did the pronunciation of them by British TV commentators sounding as though they had socks stuffed in their mouths. But that's as far as the nostalgia goes. Communism is not some forgotten musical genre from the 70s long overdue for critical reappraisal in 'Mojo' or 'Uncut'. Just ask the good people of North Korea.

I have a particular fondness for the Regency era, but as no one alive today experienced it, reading written accounts in the absence of living testimony is the closest I or any other interested party can get to it. Therefore, safe in the knowledge I'll never be put in such a position, I can comfortably declare life would be so much easier if gentlemen could still duel. Yes, it was an antiquated and illegal method of settling arguments over 'honour' even in the century that finally saw it disappear from civilian circles (i.e. the nineteenth); but it lingered for several decades as a controversial means of redressing a slight on one's character or simply ending a long-running dispute. For all the talk of Cabinet ructions today, the incumbent Government Ministers don't come close to their predecessors.

In 1809, Lord Castlereagh (Secretary of State for War and the Colonies) challenged long-time critic and Foreign Secretary George Canning to a duel on Putney Heath, a clandestine clash that resulted in amateur shot Canning being wounded in the thigh. Twenty years later during his stint at PM, the Duke of Wellington challenged the Earl of Winchilsea to a duel on Battersea Fields, sparked by the latter's opposition to Catholic Emancipation. The Duke missed whilst the Earl refrained from firing; honour was upheld. Hard to imagine today's Tory Brexiteers and Remoaners sorting out their differences in the same manner, but one cannot help but picture it as an alternative solution to political differences that conventional means seem incapable of resolving. Who knows what form Brexit might take were those involved in its implementation able to lock swords or aim pistols at the crack of dawn? Personally, there are some in this world I'd love to challenge to a duel tomorrow; and even knowing I could be mortally wounded wouldn't dissuade me, as I can think of far worse ways to go. Alas, as ever, I am a man out of time.

Ironic in a way that an item of clothing one always associates with Regency duellists – the waistcoat – has experienced an unexpected resurgence of popularity this summer courtesy of Gareth Southgate. Unusually dapper for an England manager, Southgate worked wonders with the limited means at his disposal during a World Cup in which team spirit triumphed over the Prima donna superstar; his refusal to sanction a homecoming victory parade for a team that didn't win anything is also a refreshing change that goes against the tiresome 'plucky Brit' strain of celebrating failure in the absence of success. Eddie the bloody Eagle can probably be blamed for that. Mind you, maybe we could play the Croatia game again – y'know, make it a 'People's Replay' now that we have a better understanding of how the aim is to prevent the opposition from scoring. Best of three, eh? I'm sure Gary Lineker would tweet his approval.

Something non-toxic coming out of Russia was a welcome contradiction to the ongoing narrative, though headline-writers quickly focused on another defining characteristic of the summer. While that exceptional heat-wave was viewed by some as the harbinger of the climate apocalypse, to others it was just another of those sweaty intermissions we have every few years. More people seemed concerned the nation was poised to run out of beer during the World Cup than by the fact that every summer from now on threatens to evoke the kind of comparisons with 1976 that are destined to rival Fleet Street's inevitable references to 1963 come each winter. Of course, if long hot summers are to be normalised, it sadly reduces the comical sight of red-skinned natives wincing with every step in their air-conditioned Crocs, as I should imagine most are now aware enough of what the sun can do to pale flesh to take precautions beforehand. Anyway, it's already started raining again.

I don't think the expression 'burning the *post*-midnight oil' actually exists, but I hereby invent it because it seems more applicable to the twilight zone I inhabit. Hell, a heat-wave is never conducive to a good night's sleep, for one thing; but I was still active at 3.00 or 4.00am six months ago, back when my frozen frame was dependent on a fan heater as well as an invaluable electric blanket (when I felt I ought to finally drag myself towards the mattress whose warmth is strictly artificially-induced). Therefore, I can't blame this joyless interlude devoid of all beauty on the summer. At the moment, brief bursts of creative energy just aren't enough to let the sunshine in. Look at my most recent video and be fooled into believing it's the work of a man as sharp as the blade that duellists once pierced a waistcoat with. It's not. But it's quite funny if you like that sort of thing. Anyway, I'll shut up and keep trying until I've awakened from my dream of life.

MESSAGE IN A BOTTLE
7 September 2018

I'm still alive, which surely proves I'm not spending all day watching the telly whilst not here. I don't watch much TV as it is and certainly wouldn't before 7.00 in the evening, anyway. Recently forced to upgrade by my digital supplier, I did so with little enthusiasm, though I can now 'Series Link', which is a bit like programming ye olde VCR to record a particular programme weeks in advance. It's not something I'll probably make much use of, however, as I tend to use the TV set as an effective monitor for the DVD player most of the time. And what I do like to watch is usually regarded as being of minority interest, which means it's always in danger of disappearing from the screen. The word 'minority' has different connotations where mainstream broadcasters are concerned, anyway.

The recent announcement that those oh-so wise guardians of the licence fee have decided to slash the budget of BBC Parliament – probably to finance further 'life-changing journeys' through some far-flung foreign field for a bunch of has-beens from the 80s – is typical of the Corporation's priorities when confronted by criticism: keep the crap and dispense with everything that makes it unique (see also the sales of Maida Vale and BBC Caversham, plus the regular pruning of World Service branches). Moreover, the cutting back of the Parliament channel is a blow for archival anoraks who've enjoyed numerous nights viewing unearthed real-time coverage of distant General Elections on said channel. Thankfully, most are available on YouTube now, albeit not subject to the censorious new moral regime that is constantly

194

preventing me making a penny from my own videos; anyway, it was online where I received my latest fix when sitting through the 1970 show.

Avuncular anchor Cliff Michelmore had a mouth remarkably similar to that of a frog; I kept expecting an elongated tongue to lash out and whip a fly from the nose of David Butler during the broadcast. Alas, it didn't happen, but it was an entertaining watch, all the same. A degree of civility and politeness on the part of the presenters when speaking to politicians came as a refreshing shock, particularly from Robin Day, who is still credited with a fearsome proto-Paxman reputation; and when compared to the tiresome bullishness of the 'Channel 4 News' or 'Newsnight' teams of today – behaving like prosecution barristers from their very first accusation – the less confrontational approach of Robin Day actually achieves better results from MPs not instantly on the defensive. Then again, perhaps the men from the Ministries were held in a slightly higher regard back then.

As ever with these programmes, glimpses of the general public are a priceless window onto a lost world – a bit like a recent DVD outing, the mid-70s Thames TV murder-mystery panel game, 'Whodunnit?', hosted by Jon Pertwee with regular panellists in the shape of the swaggeringly-suave Patrick Mower and the gorgeously languorous actress-cum-hotelier Anouska Hempel. At one point, a member of the public is added to the panel every week (courtesy of winning a TV Times competition), and each bears all the endearing awkwardness-on-camera absent from media-savvy millennials. Regarding the public of Election 70, however, there is additional fun to be had through spotting future faces hidden behind the floral shirts, including journalist Simon Jenkins hanging out at a swanky London night-club in a sequence that resembles a Carnaby Street pilot of 'The Hit

Man and Her' – and Gyles Brandreth whilst still a student at Oxford.

The declarations themselves are quite dramatic on occasion; though not as momentous a wipe-out as 1997, the unexpected ousting of the Wilson Government saw some impressive scalps claimed by the victors, none more so than the colourful figure of George Brown, losing his seat after 25 years. The notorious old soak managed to stay sober during the tension provoked by the recount, and Brown's losing speech was his final public address as a 'commoner', for he enjoyed a familiar elevation to the Lords almost immediately thereafter. Watching the defeat made me wonder what it must feel like to receive rejection on such a scale (Brown lost Belper by more than 2,000 votes), though I suppose it depends on how much you care for your constituents. I would imagine being rejected by just one person you love is a tougher experience than being rejected by 2,000 people you couldn't give a toss about.

Would I have more confidence in our elected representatives if the likes of Wilson, Heath, Callaghan, Castle, Jenkins, Whitelaw, Thorpe, Thatcher or Powell were amongst the candidates today? Looking at perhaps the most abysmal and incompetent Tory Government in living memory (including Major's) and then glancing across at a Labour Opposition infected with identity politics and boasting a Corbyn alternative in the likes of oily Umunna, I can only come to the conclusion I'd rather be on the 1970 electoral register than the 2018 one. I don't think I've ever had less confidence in any of them to deliver the goods than I have right now. The Brexit charade seems to sum it all up, a farce as demoralising as the ongoing soap opera in Washington. Hard not to be a cynic and simply think f**k the lot of 'em. Mind you, most days I think f**k the world and everyone in it, so I guess politicians are open goals for contempt.

Twitter can often provide a different perspective on affairs, especially if you follow incompatible participants from across the ideological spectrum. It's healthy to have your opinions challenged as well as reinforced, though even this can grate after a while. Of course, both sides highlight anything that supports their chosen narrative, so the left bigs up the Boris-is-an Islamophobe storyline whilst the right milks Jezza's anti-Semitic terrorist sympathies; alongside these headlines are smaller stories that do a similar job, though one can't help but wonder if they're being reported solely to promote an agenda as inflexible as its polar opposite. Too much exposure to it all and I come away convinced both sides of the divide are as bad as each other; and I've got enough negative energy to deal with as it is.

Unsurprisingly, I'm not feeling especially charitable towards anyone at the moment, and as public figures whose careers are in 'public life' can provoke both anger and annoyance at the best of times, I'm hardly in the right frame of mind to pen balanced assessments of their performances and, on occasion, give them the benefit of the doubt. If there's only bile in the belly, you're left with Alex Jones; if there's only petulant conviction you're right and everyone else is wrong, you're left with *Owen* Jones. And if there's no sign of a heart, you're left with Katy Hopkins. As Richard Nixon said, 'Those who hate you don't win unless you hate *them*. And then, you destroy yourself.'

I appreciate some of you may miss the days when I would write about anything in the news; I do myself. But despite my best efforts, the prospect of returning to regular posts on here still leaves me impotent. A year ago, I could write daily dispatches without breaking sweat; but a year ago I could kiss the day goodnight secure in the knowledge that everything to have constituted the day would be there for me to kiss goodnight again tomorrow. There was plenty of time to take everything for granted and wallow in the blissful complacency that comes with perceived security. Well, that security has gone now and I'm stranded on this bastard island until my eyes are able to recognise a rescue ship when they see it. I should've gone to Specsavers. But as the spirit of dark and lonely water once said to a traumatised generation, I'll be back-back-back-back-back...

CRYSTAL BALLS
15 October 2018

How much unexpected meetings or chance encounters that lead to seismic life changes are indeed down to chance or are merely inevitable moves in a preordained plan depends, I guess, on your view of man as either an autonomous animal in control of his own destiny or as a mere pawn in God's grand scheme. The Osmonds certainly fell on 'the plan' side of the argument, as the title of their 1973 concept album testified – though why 'Long-Haired Lover from Liverpool' fitted in to His big idea remains an extremely mystifying example of the Almighty moving in a very mysterious way.

Sticking with all things Merseyside, take 6 July 1957. Skiffle is the first of many teenage fads to come, and a church fête gives The Kids a chance to strum their washboards amidst the Morris dancers and a display by the City of Liverpool Police Dogs. On this occasion, The Kids are a bunch of school pals called The Quarrymen, led by a 16-year-old named John Lennon. The cocky leader of the pack shares a mutual friend with an equally overconfident adolescent called Paul McCartney; said friend introduces the most successful song-writing partnership in musical history to each other for the first time that day. And so the wheels of a cultural revolution

198

are slowly set in motion with neither party remotely aware of it. How could they be?

It's quite possible McCartney might have decided not to accept his pal's offer to visit Woolton that summer's day in 1957; after all, Macca had only just turned 15, still at a young enough age to be susceptible to other offers characteristic of a 1950s British childhood. If he'd gone fishing or train-spotting or had indulged in a jumpers-for-goalposts kick-about, the world would have kept on turning and none of these activities would have altered it, unlike the meeting at that church fête, which *did* – in many ways, for all of us. One could argue the mutual friend of Lennon & McCartney – Ivan Vaughan – was a pivotal figure in modern history, yet he could just as easily not have been. On such wafer-thin paper is history written.

The tempting 'What if?' scenario has generated many speculative and imaginative alternatives to historical events over the years: think of a novel such as Robert Harris's 'Fatherland' taking place in a parallel universe 1960s, twenty years after Nazi Germany won World War II. Counterfactual history approaches the concept with a more academic eye, though many historians see it as an essentially pointless exercise; Nazi Germany didn't win WWII, but was that always destined to be the final score on the eve of kick-off?

Certain figures whose actions changed the course of world history often appear to have led charmed lives, as though there was indeed a plan in mind for them. As Andrew Roberts highlights in his new biography of Winston Churchill, the Great British icon was born two months premature, suffered a near-fatal bout of pneumonia as a child and was stabbed as a schoolboy; he regularly diced with death as a soldier, and civilian life was punctuated by three car crashes and two plane crashes, all of which he survived along with numerous strokes and heart attacks. Pure chance or preordained?

If one believes our destinies are already mapped out for us before we even arrive in the world, one could almost adopt a petulant attitude to our apparently powerless part in directing those destinies. What's the point in trying if we're only acting out actions penned in advance anyway, being little more than marionettes whose every move is dictated by some celestial puppet master? If whatever we do makes no difference to the eventual outcome, we could consciously live a life of inactive isolation, surrendering to sloth and deliberately avoiding effort altogether. Then again, by doing so we may well be merely fulfilling a designated role after all. It's a conundrum if life seems frustratingly impervious to our attempts to improve it, as though we permanently sleep on the wrong side of the bed.

We've all retrospectively recognised moments in life when we've stood at a crossroads and chosen a specific route from several options available to us. These options could have been deliberated upon at length beforehand or we may have just thrown caution to the wind with an 'eeny meeny miny moe' moment. If the consequences of our decision fail to deliver, it's unavoidable that years later we ponder on what might have happened had we chosen one of the other options. Middle-age is especially prone to such hindsight musings, though only if we don't find what we're looking for once we get there. And, of course, there's always the nagging belief that what we *didn't* do would have turned out so much better than what we actually *did*. If only...

When constructing these parallel universe lives, it pays to pause and recall the saving graces that emerged from even the darkest of times, those times we become convinced life could have done without. In my own experience, feline and canine companions came out of a period in the 1990s I often wish I could erase from memory, yet both cat and dog long outlived its merciful end, enriching my existence for years afterwards; without that painful period, I would have been denied the joy they brought. Therefore, I accept it was necessary – my own personal 40 days and nights in the wilderness. And I'm sure we've all had them.

I've never visited a fortune-teller nor bought into their mystical shtick, not out of any inflexible opinion that they pedal pure hokum, but mainly because I genuinely have no desire to see into the future - even if it were possible. Should the crystal ball show me something I don't want to see, I'd be convinced the future is already arranged and it'd be futile me trying to change it. And feeling as though someone else is scripting that future puts one back into the worst kind of childhood mindset, trapped in a world where all-powerful beings, from parents to teachers, are in control of everything that happens to you. Your input is negligible in terms of impact compared to theirs, so why bother?

One problem with accepting the preordained notion of life as a readymade plan is that, unlike the end result of WWII, it doesn't always *go* to plan. Sometimes a luminous path ahead that certainly feels preordained as it generates good vibrations is abruptly blocked and we are rerouted against our will, back down a darker avenue as the trite 'well, it just wasn't meant to be' excuse is trotted out. One could either behave like a senior Met officer and lock one's self in one's car when confronted by an unexpected and unpleasant turn of events or one could face them head on. But the latter depends on whether or not one has faith in the possibility of a reward for doing so; and faith, like love, trust and hope, is not always the most accessible of subscriptions when life's size-nine's have your groin (and your crystal balls) in their sights. But maybe that's the fate that always awaits we fools who (like Blanche Dubois) still believe in magic...

KNIVES AND FAWKES
5 November 2018

Yeah, I remember (remember) the fifth of November. How could I forget? One fifth of November not so long ago mine eyes did see the light – to paraphrase the final speech of a late lamented orator – and this wholly secular illumination finally toppled a distant and previously unchallenged blink of elation from its long-held pole position in the memory banks. That had occurred on a sunny day in 1974 when I first mastered the tricky task of propelling myself on two wheels without falling over; alas, the applause and cheers that rang in my ears upon pedalling the short distance to liberation from the tricycle now feel as far away as its belated successor does from the bottomless pit that life decided I would be more at home in. All I can hear from here is the discharge of gunpowder in the annual celebration of a plot that failed to succeed and left us with what we have today, four-hundred and odd years later. Is that really worthy of celebration?

With so many appalling institutions to choose from, so many that were established in idealistic circumstances and have betrayed their original intent, afraid I have to hone in on the one that hogs more headlines than any other. Yes, some things in life are sacred and their betrayal cuts deeper than the sharpest scythe; but I wonder if my increasingly incurable cynicism towards our elected representatives and their motives is simply a symptom of my own personal (and undeniably unhealthy) state of mind or merely the inevitable outcome of a fairly traumatic political decade.

I know MPs are easy targets, but to be fair, they do ask for it. It's less than ten years since the Expenses' Scandal, exactly a year since the most recent 'sex scandal' (one that cost the jobs of two members of the Cabinet), and allegations of bullying within Westminster are ongoing. And I'm sure I'm not the only outside observer weary with it all. A financial crash, punitive austerity, a coalition government, two incredibly divisive referendums, the Brexit balls-up, and the endless splitting of vitriolic factions that only ever aids a divide-and-rule agenda; my gut reaction can't help but evoke the spirit of Roy Castle amending his theme song - 'generalisation, that's what you need.' I dunno. Maybe politicians just seem to be bigger bastards the longer one pays attention and the more one is inevitably let down. Even if the blatant efforts of so many to derail a democratic mandate and preserve a thoroughly rotten status quo wasn't such a classic example of why they languish amongst the lowest subspecies of the human race, it's not as though it's the only one.

Principles and morals – not exactly essential qualifications for entering the hallowed environs of Parliament these days, one concludes (if they ever were). Just take a cursory glance through the 'serious' section of Private Eye and marvel at the endless litany of obscene amounts paid to Honourable Members as company directors or corporate consultants in addition to their Westminster wages and fiddled expenses; not much belt-tightening on display, and even MPs one would generally like to credit with a bit of integrity have hardly suffered during the Age of Austerity (which, lest we forget, is now officially over). If they're not receiving back-handers from lobbyists, they're being flown out on junkets to tax havens or Middle Eastern oases by undemocratic regimes courting their favour and eager for a little influence in the corridors of power. And these regimes know how easy it is because the people they're dealing with are almost as unscrupulously immoral as they are, albeit considerably vainer and dimmer.

That kindergarten of corruption, the local council, is the breeding ground for many of those who then make the leap to the parliamentary hustings; all of the toxic trappings of Parliament are present on a smaller scale, serving as a virtual training camp for the worst Westminster can offer. Just ask the good people of Northamptonshire. At times, it's hard not to surmise that anyone seeking promotion to the political premier league from the rotten boroughs is little more than a conceited, self-aggrandising sociopath only out for themselves and prepared to ruthlessly clamber over anyone – friend or foe – to get where they want to be, essentially poison ivy to whom others are convenient trellises. *I* can't sleep at night, true; but I've no idea how most MPs do. I don't know how the majority of the mendacious hypocrites have the nerve to stand up and lecture the rest of us on how to live our lives, quite frankly. They are the least qualified members of society to do so, yet they do – constantly.

Those of us immune to the appeal of politics as a profession make friendships and alliances in life that we hope will be of long-lasting significance; we do so with no motive other than the desire to spend time in good company because we enjoy it, not because we see this company as something that can facilitate a move somewhere else, using people as a climbing frame and callously dispensing with them when they've ceased to be of any further use. If we behaved that way in daily life we'd rightly be regarded as a bit of a shit. In politics, however – as in business, which is often indistinguishable from it – such behaviour is applauded as a sign of strength, especially when it comes to government.

The unedifying backstabbing that took place in the wake of David Cameron's resignation a couple of years ago was a case in point. True, it was already difficult to warm to the likes of Boris and Gove, but the way in which they laid down their friends for their lives was indeed a telling lesson in the dark arts of party politics and should have earned both the eternal contempt they deserve. And thanks to their stint as pantomime villains, we ended up with Motherfucker Theresa – the last woman standing as the Tories re-staged the climax to 'Reservoir Dogs'. Then again, maybe the desperation that ensued when Dave departed reflected a wider crisis; maybe politicians have become worse because they're terrified they're bordering on extinction now that the world is run by corporations rather than elected representatives; maybe we're witnessing their Nero moment.

At the same time, I suppose there's an argument to be made that Parliament enables the intellectually-challenged to have something to keep them busy; after all, where else could a retarded dumpling of a redundant turd such as Chris Grayling find a role in society? He's akin to the thick third son of an old-school aristocrat, earmarked for a career in the clergy. If their actions didn't affect the lives of so many others, we could perhaps leave them to play in their Victorian Gothic nursery like the privileged special needs cases they are, safe in the knowledge they're only harming themselves. Unfortunately, they're not. Even the relatively inoffensive 'silent majority' of constituency MPs (most of whom we vote for every four or five years) may start out with high hopes and the best of intentions, but should they end up far higher than they imagined - well, as the old saying goes, all power...you know the rest. It's not for nothing that Guy Fawkes was once referred to as 'the last man to enter Parliament with honest intentions.'

Of course, I may well warm a little towards the current crop once they're out of politics. Portillo I find occasionally engaging as a presenter, and I even admit to quite enjoying Balls and Osborne's Saint & Greavsie routine last Election night. But, as stated previously, right now I'm not in a position to pass judgement with balance and fairness on those who raise my spiky hackles, so perhaps it's probably for the best that I withdraw and leave the nation to roll over as Universal Credit rolls out. Maybe we're all Nero now.

MAD AS HELL
19 November 2018

Anger – there's a lot of it about. In a young man behaving badly, it allegedly constitutes part of his kicking-against-the-pricks obnoxious charisma; over-40, however, and you're in Victor Meldrew territory. Perhaps by then you're supposed to have settled down and accepted your miserable lot because you can't beat the system; any sign of continued exasperation with The Man is merely the mark of a grumpy old git. And as grumpy old gits outnumber the young today, they're not the most popular members of society; after all, weren't they supposed to have delivered Brexit (or so the story goes)?

Yet, take a detour into social media, supposedly the chosen forum for The Kids, and you'll find anger appears to be the prime vehicle for expression, whatever your age or even sex. Whether you're a snowflake student seeking to no-platform someone you disagree with, a yummy mummy infuriated by your rival at the school gates, a sci-fi nerd incensed by the latest entry in your favourite movie franchise, or an Instagram pouter compelled to 'fat-shame' the It Girl of the moment, anger is in abundance. And even if you refrained from commenting, just ask yourself if any tweet or post made you angry today. It must have been a rare day indeed if none did.

So much of what we encounter online appeals to the emotions rather than the intellect, a fast-track to a gut reaction which is perhaps a defining characteristic of our response to today's numerous issues.

Step back out of cyberspace, though, and anger is just as prevalent. Ethnic adolescents being stopped and searched by the police; redundant white males navigating the benefits trap; distraught parents confronted by the PC intransigence of social services; touchline fathers convinced that goal was offside; whining Remoaners/foaming-at-the-mouth Brexiteers; motorists, pedestrians, supermarket shoppers – it's as though modern society, which is supposed to be such an improvement on the days when we were primitive savages living in huts and dying from the Plague (i.e. the 1970s), has oddly exacerbated anger rather than sedated it, spawning a strain of tourette's that afflicts the collective population of the western world. The great panaceas that corporations have developed to make life easier than it apparently used to be has instead created endless sources of frustration; our seeming inability to resolve them can make veritable mountains out of trivial molehills.

Whenever the issue of widespread drug abuse surfaces as a topic, the 'why do people do it' question always seems to me a no-brainer; if our wonderful system provided the same kind of blissful release that comes from a spliff or a syringe, there'd be no need to turn to an illegal alternative. Yes, millions switch on the bloody 'X-Factor' for an escape into voluntary mental paralysis; but for just as many that toxic breed of contrived gladiatorial entertainment is as much a part of the problem as the fastidious speed camera or the pensioner plodding in the middle of the pavement or the letter from British Gas claiming you owe them money when you don't or the computer crashing without warning. Sometimes, these little annoyances group together and conspire to do their stuff simultaneously; when this happens, it can seem like the whole world is against us. And we get angry.

One only has to scroll down three or four comments on yer average YouTube video for discourse to descend into racist name-calling. A typical example would be some archive and utterly innocuous footage of a London street from half-a-century ago; most marvel at the minimal amount of traffic or the fascinating fashions, then somebody comments on the absence of 'coloured' faces and all hell breaks loose. Anger again. Same goes for the response to spoof Twitter accounts such as the brilliantly satirical Titania McGrath, following on from similar spoof accounts of posh SJWs that were taken seriously – and literally – by those bereft of a sense of humour and ended up being deleted by the powers-that-be as a consequence. People are becoming so accustomed to taking things at face value that shades of grey don't compute. I guess the easy default button today is simply to get angry, even when it's blatantly obvious someone's just taking the piss.

Granted, there are undoubtedly moments concerning more important issues where anger is understandable. Anyone who has the stomach for merely a cursory glance at the PM's draft Brexit withdrawal 'deal', which leaves this country more subservient to the EU than it was under actual membership, cannot help but feel angry. Regardless of which side of the great divide one resides on, it's hard not to come away from such a pitiful (not to say cynical) white flag feeling as though calls for a second referendum are meaningless when we're essentially remaining anyway. It certainly gives every appearance of being a betrayal of a democratic mandate on an unprecedented scale (and final confirmation that our voice counts for sod all in the corridors of power), but what can any of us do about it? Sweet FA, mate. How many marched to stop the invasion of Iraq way back when? It doesn't matter because it didn't make the slightest bit of difference. So, what's left for us but anger? Unfortunately, anger is bloody exhausting.

The recent upsurge of interest in old-school hobbies like knitting or sewing – ones still negatively associated by more than one generation with blue-rinsed nanas – suggests the novelty of an archaic pastime and its defiantly non-twenty-first century ability to reduce blood pressure has a Zen-like appeal for some. And, while such a sedate interlude might be a little too twee for everyone, the allure of something so alien to the instant nature of contemporary click-bait culture is unarguable. If hi-tech creature-comforts can often increase our tendency towards anger, perhaps it's no surprise their simpler predecessors are attractive as a means of calming us down.

This has happened before, though; think of the 60s Rock Gods who, having purchased the recognisable symbols of success that the consumerist conveyor belt had prepared earlier, suddenly realised mansions and Rolls Royce's didn't actually make their lives that much more fulfilled. They then rejected these flashy trappings and began dressing like hirsute hobos as they got back to the garden. Yes, they had the luxury of being able to afford an approximation of rustic simplicity, but this abrupt embrace of nature then bled into the wider movement for self-sufficiency that has proved enduring as a rat-race opt-out, despite Margot and Jerry's objections.

Of course, reclining in the arms of a beautiful woman (or non-binary individual of your choice) could suffice as a preferable approach to anger management. The causes of anger can be rendered irrelevant when mankind's oldest notion of escapism intervenes, and whilst there may still be plenty to be angry about beyond the bedroom, none of it seems that significant in the heat of passion. So, is that really the reason for the abundance of anger in 2018 – not enough people are getting laid? Well, I guess that depends on how much you value the purely physical over potentially spiritual. Add love to the sex mix and you're elevated to a much higher level, one that outlasts the momentary gratification of base lust. Base lust is a much more accurate metaphor for the present day, however. We want the world and we want it now, as someone once said a long time ago. Maybe *that's* the problem.

LAST WORD
6 December 2018

What a year. What – *a year?* Nah. Not so much a year, more an involuntary exercise in extended despair lit by an SAD lamp due to the no-show sunrise; or to be precise, a perpetual bleak afternoon in mid-February with a blinding-white, cloudless sky keeping the soil hard and the grass grey. This is the year that never was, the year written-off before it even began – strangled in the womb once the first domino fell. I knew it would be the longest, hardest slog of all, and I was right. A powerless witness to the moment Arcadia became Hiroshima - unleashing many a dormant demon in the process - I haplessly tried to turn back every stopped clock; but this was the catalyst for collapse, when joy, beauty, happiness and hope were so utterly obliterated from the landscape that it's often been impossible to imagine them ever resurfacing. Farewell, 2018. It hasn't been nice knowing you.

To anyone thinking 'he used to be good, but he's really lost it this year', welcome to the last word (all being well) from 'the breakdown chronicles' – and if you're prepared to walk in my shoes for seven more paragraphs, this is the post for you; if not, look away now. Of course, telling it like it is with prominent warts precludes sugar-coating, but we're all

210

grownups here, and we all know the world can often be a very unpleasant place – especially when the sparks depart our own little corner of it. Okay. Are you sitting uncomfortably? Then we'll begin...

A bud beheaded before it flowered has all the skewered promise of Amy, Jimi or Kurt curtailed in haste and in waste; in other words, it's January and I'm resident at a crime scene. I'm allocating possessions to the most deserving, along with money in the event of an event anticipated; do I box them or bag them to make their distribution easier for those entrusted with the unenviable task? I owe them something at least. No doubt they'll be expecting the call, anyway. The daily testimony in ink has been superseded by on-camera monologues conducted in varying stages of inebriation; I presume they'll be viewed as posthumous documents of decline now, with the private made public because it doesn't matter anymore. The walls inch closer, the light fades, the avenues of pleasure are cordoned-off, and preparations are made to add another insignificant name to the statistics. You're on your own, kid.

A Wilde thing graces the calendar's second page, though his entrance is unexpected when it comes. I never thought I'd see Dorian Gray's daddy. How come I'm still here? Cowardice or hubris? Anyway, internalised trauma is manifested as obsessively recording the dead and discarded of a destiny denied in prose, verse and video – distracting anal admin as the Devil draws up work rotas for any sign of idle hands. The box-set suggests similarly sad and unshared salvation in escapist down-time retrophilia, with pretend friends opening a portal I can peer into but never enter. Joni M and Gainsbourg C succeed winter's mellotron as spring gatecrashes the exterior whilst the interior remains comatose, recycling redundant anniversaries as imaginary porn plays on a flammable reel, burning holes in the fabric of magic.

The creeping menace of the next blow – which feels inevitable if the established narrative is to be maintained – instils a permanent fear of tomorrow that makes retirement from the day wholly undesirable, provoking as it does the dawn of another energy-sapping round. Twitchy tossing and turning hours pass, then off we go again; three black coffees and seconds out. Ding-bloody-ding. Platforms that provided an outlet and spawned an audience are devoid of appeal in this atmosphere, as are all the stories that come and go free from comment; everything seems so immense and so exhausting in contemplation, let alone action. Every scream is released into a vacuum as the depth of the trough is rarely revealed, for the few prepared to listen may realise the magnitude of the mission and pull out prematurely, as though fearful of catching a contagious disease. Their absence would make a difference; nobody new can be trusted with such information now, nor can they ever again.

Backseat passengers strapped into a driverless vehicle (destination unknown) blub like babies at the slightest trigger. Too much is imbued with heavyweight memory that beats with the intensity of the eternally cherished. Aural (and visual) stimulation stokes the sadness without warning, which is why isolation is essential. Do you want the world to see what a wreck you really are, always one step away from dissolving into melancholy mush? Embarrassment and shame are obscured by necessary niceties when company calls, the false impression a blend of survival and denial; moreover, it serves as a safeguard should the judgemental perceive the trivial when confronted by the uncomfortable. Occasional online missives also manufacture the illusion all is well and that the waspish edges remain sharper than a serpent's tooth.

The lives of others lie on social media; I lie of mine in person too, dining alone as a flabby cadaver rotting from the inside.

Comrade Smirnoff and Monsieur Chardonnay uphold their position as purveyors of desperate elixirs despite another spirit - that of '76 - attempting a useless resuscitation when the soul's animation has been suspended; heat is a frivolous, ill-fitting irritant, whereas cold makes sense when the sole source of warmth is withdrawn with the chilling ease of stardust drifting out the door. The unseasonal fog has to be slogged through like the evening void and the silent night, even if there is still no convincing reason as to why. The ghosts in my machine continue to choke on the ashes of deceased desire, raked over and analysed with the kind of forensic precision Poirot would be proud of, as though cracking the riddle will alter the outcome. No. The present is the past with all the best bits edited out; the future can go f**k itself – as can earthly bread when heavenly bread is all that matters. Mourning hasn't broken; black is black, whatever the weather.

Apparently, it's another month, but it's irrelevant because nothing has changed bar the world outside the window; the seasons switch with the same inexplicable abruptness of an architect becoming an assassin or reality reduced to mere dream. The kindness of those to whom we are now strangers was too good for too long (talkin' 'bout my aberration), and life is a missing persons report – missing persons, missing pleasures, missing everything. It has hatched a hard-boiled egg of a cynic, one who doesn't subscribe to the conveyor belt. After all, why search for a silver medal when you've held a gold? Meanwhile, as I'm down, my teeth are there to be kicked-in and various eager parties line-up for a penalty shoot-out. DWP? YT? Let 'em get on with it. What do I care? Truths are lies, lies are truths, and fake is the news. This isn't Strawberry Fields, but nothing is real, all the same.

The pavement blanket is now ginger and crispy underfoot, but the romantic air cannot penetrate the permafrost, regardless of the gorgeous spectrum plummeting from the branches as they strip for the imminent full circle. Burying a lovely old life and enduring a horrible new one, these are the wilderness years condensed into twelve months – I hope; twelve more months of this and I am spent. But when the worst thing that can happen to you has happened, nothing can ever hurt you again, right? At the same time, anyone expecting me to regenerate into the irritatingly upbeat Tommy Steele of 'Half a Sixpence' as of midnight is residing in Cuckoo Land; such delusional optimism is naive at best and wilfully ignorant at worst. Having said that, the Reaper no longer looms quite so large on the wordsmith wish-list; and, lest we forget, a quartet of hippies from LA, Texas, Salford and Toronto once acknowledged that we have no choice but to carry on – so fingers crossed that when next we meet I'm in a better place...if I can find one...

9 781689 841535